Twenty-first Century Feminism

Twenty-first Century Feminism

Forming and Performing Femininity

Edited by

Claire Nally
Northumbria University, UK

Angela Smith
University of Sunderland, UK

First published 2015 by
PALGRAVE MACMILLAN

Palgrave Macmillan in the UK is an imprint of Macmillan Publishers Limited,
registered in England, company number 785998, of Houndmills, Basingstoke,
Hampshire RG21 6XS.

Palgrave Macmillan in the US is a division of St Martin's Press LLC,
175 Fifth Avenue, New York, NY 10010.

Palgrave Macmillan is the global academic imprint of the above companies
and has companies and representatives throughout the world.

Palgrave® and Macmillan® are registered trademarks in the United States,
the United Kingdom, Europe and other countries.

ISBN 978–1–137–49284–5

This book is printed on paper suitable for recycling and made from fully
managed and sustained forest sources. Logging, pulping and manufacturing
processes are expected to conform to the environmental regulations of the
country of origin.

A catalogue record for this book is available from the British Library.

Library of Congress Cataloging-in-Publication Data
Twenty-first century feminism : forming and performing femininity / [edited by]
    Claire Nally, Northumbria University, UK ; Angela Smith, University of
    Sunderland, UK.
        pages   cm
    Includes bibliographical references and index.
    ISBN 978–1–137–49284–5 (hardback)
    1. Feminism and mass media.   2. Feminism—History—21st century.
    3. Women in mass media.   I. Nally, Claire, 1979– editor.
    II. Smith, Angela, 1969– editor.
    P96.F46T94 2015
    305.42009′05—dc23   2014049657

Contents

Illustrations

Figures

Tables

Acknowledgements

Grateful thanks to Susie Lau and Tavi for permission to use the images in Chapter 4, and to Street Editorial Office, Tokyo, for permission to reproduce the images in Chapter 7. Images in Chapter 3 are courtesy of Channel 4.

Contributors

Editors

Claire Nally is Senior Lecturer in Twentieth-Century English Literature at the University of Northumbria. She specializes in gender and subculture, as well as Irish literature and culture. Her first book, *Envisioning Ireland*, was published in 2009, and her subsequent book, *Advertising, Literature and Print Culture in Ireland, 1891–1922* was written with John Strachan (2012). Claire has also co-edited *Naked Exhibitionism: Gendered Performance and Public Exposure* (2013) with Angela Smith. Her most recent work is on neo-Victorianism, as well as gender and sexuality in Goth subcultures. She has published articles on burlesque, is an author for *The Edinburgh Companion to Critical Theory* (edited by Stuart Sim) and is currently writing a monograph on gender and steampunk. With Angela Smith, she is the co-editor of the I. B. Tauris International Library of Gender and Popular Culture.

Angela Smith is Reader in Language and Culture at the University of Sunderland. She has published widely in the areas of gender, media discourse and politics. With Claire Nally, she is co-editor of the I. B. Tauris International Library of Gender and Popular Culture.

Contributors

Jennifer Anyan is Principal Lecturer and Programme Group Leader in Media and Fashion Styling at Southampton Solent University. Her multidisciplinary research practice engages in a dialogue with the construction of personal identity and styled image through the production of artwork and critical text. Her work has been exhibited widely, most recently a solo exhibition: Embodied Memories which was commissioned by the John Hansard Gallery.

Anne Burns is a PhD candidate at the Loughborough University School of Art. Her thesis examines how women's photographic self-representations are used on social media to enact practices of gender discipline. Whether defining the 'authentic' self, proscribing the 'duckface' expression or deriding the use of selfies, popular discourse in relation to women's photographs can be seen to embody the normalization of regulation, presented as a participatory form of entertainment. She writes a blog at thecarceralnet.wordpress.com and has contributed to the Either/And project http://eitherand.org/reconsidering-amateur -photography/creepshots-candids-and-amateur-photographer-respon/ and been featured on Photomediations Machine photomediations machine.net/2014/02/15/selfies-and-the-numbers-game/

Leslie Heywood is Professor of English at the State University of New York, Binghamton. With Jennifer Drake, she developed the first academic formulation of third wave feminism in the US in *Third Wave Agenda,* and she edited that subject's first reference work, *The Women's Movement Today.* She is the author of many books on women, gender and sport, including *Built to Win: The Female Athlete as Cultural Icon, Bodymakers: A Cultural Anatomy of Women's Bodybuilding* and *Pretty Good for a Girl.*

Makiko Iseri is a PhD candidate in gender studies based in the School of Media, Film and Music at University of Sussex. Her current interests involve queer theory, disability theory and cultural studies to problematize political discourse and visual representation of the body associated with chronic and progressive illness, pain or discomfort, and death.

Karen Sturgeon-Dodsworth is a PhD student at Leeds Metropolitan University. Her thesis is on representing the past, specifically looking at gender and sexuality in neo-Victorian films and books, and adaptations of nineteenth-century novels. Other research interests are contemporary women's writing, adaptations and, most recently, looking at the relationship between science and literature.

Rosie White is Senior Lecturer in Contemporary Literature, Theory and Popular Culture at Northumbria University. Her research interests include the novels of Michele Roberts, violent women in popular fiction, film and television, and representations of women spies in popular culture. Her monograph *Violent Femmes: Women as Spies in Popular Culture* was published in 2008 and she is currently developing work on women and television comedy.

1
Introduction

Angela Smith

This edited collection explores many aspects of just what it is to be female in the twenty-first century. By studying the social, cultural and technological changes that have influenced this, these essays contextualize feminism and femininity in a range of global locations. Although this collection of essays will examine developments in femininity in the early part of this century, there are many links back to the emergence of second wave feminism nearly half a century before, and the huge technological and social changes of the twentieth century that continue to influence women's lives, such as in the obsessive attention paid to the sexualized female body. While we can refer to the early twenty-first century as being part of the 'postfeminist' era, we can also see traces of an emerging new or 'fourth wave' feminist period coming through the use of Web 2.0 as women join up online to raise their voices to campaign for greater equality. In this collection, we will examine how women are open to ever-increasing scrutiny of their bodies and behaviours through the affordances of mass media, and while some exploit such attention for commercial gain, such as celebrities and artists, others find themselves open to humiliation, ridicule and even threats of physical violence such as found on Twitter. For example, the body that steps outside of stereotypes is celebrated, as found in the quirky world of Japanese pop music, the popularity of which has been disseminated globally through the reach of Web 2.0. The attention paid to female bodily performance is also analysed through a discussion of women in comedy, where parody and self-referentiality are in evidence to counter the criticisms of non-standard bodies as found in make-over shows. Mass media exploitation can be experienced by

1

others as having a darker side, through unlicensed use of their images for negative effect. Film and literature also show changes in the representation of twenty-first century femininity, explored here through a study of neo-Victorian fiction. While neo-Victorian fiction often espouses a radical recovery of lost female voices (the criminalized woman such as the prostitute or the suicide, the lesbian experience, deviancy, disability), we might also note that some texts produced in the twenty-first century point to a less optimistic view of female empowerment.

Attention to the female body and the judgement of its perceived perfections and imperfections has a long history. In her study of classical Hollywood films, Laura Mulvey's 1975 highly influential analysis of the psychodynamic relationship between spectator and text argued that priority is given to the masculine perspective both narratively and visually. The female characters are represented in terms of their 'to-be-looked-at-ness', a view which can also give pleasure to female viewers who can admire the dress or style of a female star (Gledhill, 1991). The various discussions relating to Mulvey's argument nevertheless acknowledge that the female body is one that is looked at and judged more than the male body. Myra Macdonald (1995, p. 193) points to the fact that historically the body has been 'much more integral to the formation of identity for women than for men'. It is not the body, she argues, but the codifying of the body into structures of appearance that culturally shapes and moulds what it means to be 'feminine'. Women have long been encouraged to view their bodies as being intrinsically related to sexual desirability. If we look at paintings of women in various historical periods, we can see how the ideal female body has changed over the years, from the full and well-rounded Renaissance woman to the material roundness cinched into an hour-glass silhouette in the Victorian age. The corset has frequently been vaunted as an example of social constraints and the ways in which women's bodies have been managed, but it is far from representing a monolithic practice. Indeed, as Valerie Steele has observed, 'it was a situated practice that meant different things to different people at different times' (Steele, 2001, p. 1). In contemporary discourses it is a slippery signifier: an 'ironic, postmodern manipulation of sexual stereotypes' (ibid., p. 176). Certainly the corseted shape gave way to more fluid lines as the constraints of women in society diminished after the First World War, with the boyish flapper image of the 1920s embodying the shifting roles of women in society. Conversely, the aftermath of the Second World War saw women who had gained enormous freedoms by taking on men's work during the war being constrained once more by corsetry to produce the 'New Look' of the 1950s. This rapidly gave way in the 1960s to the more slender 'Twiggy' look, where corsets vanished from the everyday wardrobe of women to be replaced by a slender body draped in ever-diminishing lengths of fabric. This slender body has remained the ideal female shape ever since, and can be linked to an emerging culture of post-war affluence that ended the association between thinness and poverty. This can be aligned with the rise of the diet industry and gym culture. Weight Watchers was set up in the US in 1963, establishing itself in Britain in 1967, and eventually was followed by the Heinz food company developing a highly profitable diet food franchise in the 1990s. In Foucault's theory of the body as a central location in the context of power (1980), we can see how the contradictory desires to indulge and pamper associated with post-war affluence are in conflict with the need to engage in bodily discipline through exercise. Women were persuaded that the traditionally male leisure activity of physical exercise was necessary to maintain their sexual attractiveness. Of the early proponents of female gym culture, Jane Fonda in the 1980s is the best known with her promotion of group aerobic classes. She promoted the soon-accepted notion of women working out in groups with other women. As Susan Willis points out, the celebrity gym culture that gave rise to such classes makes it difficult to separate the exercise routines from the rituals of appropriate dress and self-presentation. She says, 'for women, poised body line and flexed muscles are only half the picture. Achieving the proper workout look requires several exercise costumes, special no-smudge makeup, and an artfully understated hairdo' (1990, p. 7). This gym culture, with its emphasis on the sexualized body, is discussed in Chapter 2 by Heywood in her analysis of CrossFit, demonstrating that such focus has continued into the twenty-first century. She draws on the notion of gaze as being central to gym culture, with the female body continuing to be sexualized in a way that distinguishes it from the male body.

The 1980s was not only a time for the redefinition of the female body through disciplined diet and exercise; it also saw the arrival of new freedoms for women to experiment with dress and personal style. The second wave feminists of the 1970s had largely followed Simone de Beauvoir's description of female fashion as a form of 'bondage' (1972, p. 548) which effectively subjected women to lives as sexualized beings who were governed by the sexual desire of men. Thus 1970s feminists who rejected fashionable 'feminine' attire came to be characterized as dungaree-wearing, asexual beings who were open to anti-feminist mockery in the popular press that continues to be a legacy into the twenty-first century. By the 1980s this view had shifted, with critics such as Rosalind Coward arguing that any woman who rejected fashion was essentially marking herself as being sexually conservative (1984). The emergence of 'postfeminism' in the late 1980s is coupled with youthful playfulness of dressing with 'a self-conscious awareness of the dislocation between image and identity epitomized also in the 1980s' female music performers such as Bananarama or…Madonna' (McRobbie, 1989, p. 49). This collocation of youth and playfulness tied to celebrity is something we continue to see as a positive aspect of fashion in the twenty-first century, as we see in Anyan's discussion of fashion blogs and Iseri's analysis of Japanese *kawaii*.

The period following the main activism of second wave feminism has eventually emerged in the rather tangled, often contradictory discourses of postfeminism from the late 1980s. Postfeminism has been seen as signalling a generational shift in feminist thinking and in an understanding of the social relations between genders beyond the traditional feminist politics which saw a supposed threat to hetero-sexual relationships. As Judith Stacey (1987, p. 8) identified early in this process, we can see postfeminism as a cyclical process of femi-nist rejuvenation, emerging after the momentous and systematized 'waves' of feminist activism and politics of earlier in the twentieth century. This, she argues, can be discussed as a 'post revolutionary' shift away from the collective mobilization that characterized first and second wave feminism towards a more individualized discourse. In this moving away from the shifting advances in feminism in the 1970s and early 1980s, postfeminism can thus be seen as feminism's 'coming of age' (Brooks, 1997, p. 4), where by the early part of the twenty-first century the lucrative 18–34 female market comprised

a generation that had grown up taking for granted the feminist vic-tories won by their mothers and thus for whom feminism exists at

the level of popular commonsense rather than at the level of theo-
retic abstraction. This is a generation who have found that despite
the best efforts of feminists, you cannot just wish femininity away,
relegate it to the dustbin of history as the 'bad other' of feminism.
This is the generation for whom 'having it all' means not giving
things up but struggling to reconcile our feminist desires with our
feminine desires.

(Moseley and Reed, 2002, p. 238)

Stéphanie Genz (2009), in her discussion of postfeminism, describes
the common threads that run through this as promoting the notion
of female 'empowerment' through 'choice' and 'freedom'. As Sarah
Projansky has shown, there are many strands to postfeminism,
strands which often appear contradictory as the 'girl power' ladette
(or, in Angela McRobbie's term, the phallic girl (2009)) stands in
opposition to the neo-traditional feminist domestic goddess. Initially, the 'girl power' strand was dominant in society and in the
media in the 1990s where it was embodied by the Spice Girls.
As Rosalind Gill points out, 'femininity is a bodily property; the
shift between objectification and subjectification, the emphasis on
self-surveillance, monitoring and discipline' (2007, p. 149) and simply sees female bodily maintenance as continuing, but with the
gaze more readily attracted in a knowing way. In her discussion of
postfeminism, Angela McRobbie comments on the view that by the
late 1990s advertisers regularly drew on familiarity with 'political cor-
rectness' in appearing to respond with sexualized images of women
that 'reacted against the seemingly tyrannical regime of feminist puri-
tanism' (2009, p. 17). As she observes, such images 'seem to suggest
it is permissible, once again, to enjoy looking at the bodies of beautiful women'. In this way, younger viewers of such adverts, whether
male or female, are generationally separated from the second wave
feminists who drew attention to such sexualization and, educated in
irony and visually literate, these viewers are not angered by such sexualization but instead can appreciate its many layers. Thus anyone
who finds such sexualized imagery offensive is liable to be labelled
prudish.

However, Imelda Whelehan warns of the dangers of such
behaviour, where 'vulgarity and sexual objectification of men is supposed to pass for sexual self-determination [and] there are knowing

lampoons of traditional feminine concerns such as dieting, personal adornment [and] pleasing men' (Whelehan, 2000, p. 9). She goes on to warn, the 'ladette offers the most shallow model of gender equality; it suggests that women could or should adopt the most anti-social and pointless of "male" behaviour as a sign of empowerment. The Wonderbra, unsurprisingly, remains the essential style statement for a wannabe ladette' (ibid). Whelehan's rather pessimistic view of the ladette is one that is tied into the visual appearance of the women involved, particularly as Whelehan states, the sexualized body. As Anne Burns's article in Chapter 5 of this collection shows by drawing on Mulvey's work, the celebration of the female body through sexualized 'selfies' can be used in highly damaging ways when there is a refusal to see these images as empowering or even knowingly ironic.

By the early part of the twenty-first century, this playfulness with the male gaze, whether empowering or delusional, had shifted in its dominance with the resurgence of a more traditional form of feminism which favours the cult of the perfect housewife who chose to stay at home or juggle childcare and domestic bliss with one of the career roles that the second wave political activism had ensured would be available to her (see Smith, 2013). Susan Faludi had identified this 'back-to-the-home movement' as early as the mid-1980s, describing this as 'a recycled version of the Victorian fantasy that a "new cult of domesticity" was bringing droves of women home' (1992, p. 77). This new traditionalism, Genz and Brabon suggest, 'centralises a woman's "choice" to retreat from the public sphere and abstain from paid work in favour of family values. Severing its previous associations with drudgery and confinement, the domestic sphere is redefined and resignified as a domain of female autonomy and independence' (2009, p. 58). However, just as the cult of the 'Angel in the House' in the Victorian period or, more recently, the 1950s saw the housewife as a repository of serene beauty, the neo-traditionalist woman is likewise characterized as the 'yummy mummy' or the 'domestic goddess' as personified by the incredibly glamorous television cook Nigella Lawson. Thus what is remarkable about all the strands of postfeminism, particularly the 'ladette' and its generationally different 'neo-traditional' strands, is the continued emphasis on female sexualization. The twenty-first century re-imagining of Victorian female heroes in film and literature is considered here in Sturgeon-Dodsworth's discussion of the Sherlock Holmes films of Guy Ritchie and the various neo-Victorian novels (Chapter 8). She offers an analysis which reveals the tension between the empowered, active female of the twenty-first century and the more traditional female containment that is at the heart of much neo-traditional femininity.

Where second wave feminism was characterized by the impetus to remove sexual desire from the female appearance in order to gain a more serious, earnest equality with men, postfeminism strongly promotes the idea of feminism and femininity not being incompatible and thus sexualization of the female body being a viable choice. As Whelehan and others have argued, this choice is often something that emerges from celebrity culture where female body image is governed by male executives, and is found in Iseri's discussion of Japanese *kawaii* (Chapter 7). When this is co-opted by mainstream culture, the sexualized image becomes a 'choice' by way of emulation. Those who do not make this choice are regarded as being unfashionable, labelled frumpy or dowdy. When this is linked to body image, the woman who does not maintain her body is likely to be labelled as frigid or, at best, unsexy, as Smith's chapter here shows (Chapter 3). By the early part of the twenty-first century, this had further been linked to commercialization. Where the 1970s saw the rise of female aerobic classes and then gym culture, the quick-fix to the imperfect body came in the form of easy access to cosmetic surgery, particularly breast enhancement or, as it is more commonly referred to in British culture (in an attempt to make it appear less medical), the 'boob job'. Who needed to follow a boring, tyrannous diet when you could simply have excess fat removed by a process known as liposuction, or more radically a 'gastric band' could be fitted to stop you from eating? In fact, the British Association of Aesthetic Plastic Surgeons reported in February 2014 that there had been a 17% rise in the number of cosmetic procedures carried out in the UK in 2013 compared with the previous year and that in the UK alone the cosmetic surgery industry went from being worth £750 million in 2005 to a forecast £3.6 billion by 2015 (Gallagher, 2014). The multiplicity of such quick-fixes to the body is also found in the unstoppable rise of consumer culture elsewhere, with cheap clothing being readily available on the high street and online. Both bodily perfection and clothed attractiveness are dealt with in the chapters in this book. For example, the shift to a discourse of choice coupled with increased commercialization has led to the large number of make-over shows emerging on our TV screens in the early twenty-first century, where individual women (90% of cosmetic surgery cases in the UK are women) are seen to have 'failed' if they do not live up to expectations of female attractiveness. The development of Web 2.0 has also affected the way in which women are judged. For example, the fashion blogs discussed by Anyan (Chapter 4) show how judgements can be supportive or more moderated. This is taken to a more extreme form of humiliation and bullying by the online criticisms levelled at women whose 'selfies' are made available online without their permission (Burns, Chapter 5). In all these cases, it is often women who are the judges, showing how the male gaze that Mulvey demonstrated has been internalized by a generation who are newly empowered to pass judgement on others through the affordances of recent technological developments.

The emergence of fourth wave feminism towards the end of the first decade of the twenty-first century partly ameliorates the pessimism hinted at by some of the essays in this collection. As White's discussion of actor/comedian Miranda Hart shows (Chapter 6), female empowerment can be found through the knowing exploitation of a very non-stereotypical female body and behaviour through the medium of comedy. While there is still an underlying move to revert to traditional feminine stereotypes, whether in film and literature or in real life, the increasing widespread use of Web 2.0 has helped a new generation of feminist activism to take root. Using social media such as Twitter and Facebook, campaigns such as @EverdaySexism's #Shoutingback have encouraged people to reject the sort of violations of personal space meted out in public, primarily to women, through cat-calling and sexual suggestions by strangers as well as quieter examples of gender stereotyping (see Higgins and Smith 2014). This hashtag has been used to 'name and shame' perpetrators of 'everyday sexism' and has also successfully led to the removal of gender segregation of magazines in large outlets in the UK such as Tesco and WH Smith, which have also stopped selling the more extreme lads' mags such as *Loaded* and *FHM*. The feminist activist Caroline Criado Perez (co-founder of The Women's Room and founder of the Week Woman blog) received a wave of misogynistic abuse and rape threats on Twitter in the summer of

2013, following her high-profile participation in the successful campaign to have women's achievements feature on English bank notes. This engendered several other campaigns (such as @misogynyonline) whose objective was to foreground the negative treatment of women online. Laura Bates, the founder of @EverydaySexism, initially sought to highlight the small, generally unremarkable incidences of sexism in society (Bates, 2013). What the essays in this collection seek to do is examine how far feminism has gone in countering gender inequality while also showing that femininity remains central to the judgement of women in ways that ultimately underline Bates's initial dissatisfaction. The variety of contexts in the studies found in this collection offers an insight into how society and technology have influenced the development of feminism in this century in a global context where national boundaries have become more fluid. This fluidity is characterized by the reach of the world wide web, the global film industry, international business networks and media franchises, but also the global impact of economic crises experienced from 2007 onwards. In such a globalized context, the impact of feminism and the developments in it since the beginning of the twenty-first century are wide-reaching. The essays here seek to shed light on some of these contexts and offer insights into how and why such developments have taken place.

In Chapter 2, we start with a discussion of gendered bodies in gym culture by Leslie Heywood. The history of representation of the female athlete has been cyclic, from the 'babes' and 'muscle molls' of the early twentieth century to the 'hotness' quotients assigned in the twenty-first. What has remained consistent is that traditionally feminine athletes are idealized and more 'masculine' athletes denigrated, with a few notable exceptions in the 1940s and 1990s, and with many female athletes participating in the 'feminine apologetic': presenting as traditionally feminine to counteract the perceptions that sport participation is 'masculinizing'. As Heywood argues, though somewhat varied, the current representational frame has become more conservative since the 1990s, but as her analysis of representation in women's CrossFit culture shows, sports in which there is an emphasis on participation as distinct from competition create an alternative reality where body expectations and ideals tend to be non-normative, and 'real', functional bodies are idealized. She offers a case study of an alternative ideal in CrossFit culture to the hyperfemininity of athletes idealized in mainstream representations such as those in *ESPN Magazine.*

This bodily presentation of femininity is taken further by Angela Smith in Chapter 3 in her discussion of the way in which fashion make-over shows have changed in their approach to female participants over the course of the first decade of the twenty-first century. Make-over television shows, primarily aimed at women, have become mainstream in the course of this century. As we saw above, while postfeminism is often represented as embodying a discourse of 'empowerment', 'freedom' and 'choice', the underlying purpose of such shows appears to be that the participants have made the 'wrong choice' and are thus in need of stern guidance to enable full empowerment to be experienced. Smith suggests that the way in which choices are promoted in such shows seems to pay very little attention to the 'freedom to choose' as endorsed by postfeminist discourses, and the participants have to be forced into making the 'right choice' in clothing, hair and make-up on their way to achieving the necessary empowerment through feminine appearance. Thus the underlying impetus is to conform rather than enact free choice. Programmes such as *What Not to Wear* have been the subject of academic research, including that by Angela McRobbie (2009) and Gareth Palmer (2004) who have both scrutinized the school-girl bullying strategies embodied in these programmes. In more recent years, as Smith suggests, a less overtly bullying approach has been adopted by hosts of similar make-over shows, particularly those hosted by Gok Wan (*How to Look Good Naked,* etc) yet there remains an underlying form of ritual humiliation. Using critical discourse analysis, Smith explores the interaction between hosts and participants in two similar programmes from 2006 and 2009. This allows for a wider discussion of the possible reasons for such a shift in strategy while demonstrating that the underlying discourse of empowerment through 'prescribed' clothing remains.

In Chapter 4, Jennifer Anyan examines the intersection of fashion imagery and technological advances in her discussion of fashion blogs. She argues that metamodernism has been characterized as a pendulum swing between poles of enthusiasm and irony, hope and melancholy, naïvety and knowingness, empathy and apathy, wholeness and fragmentation (Vermeulen and Akker, 2010). Within the context of metamodernism, Anyan looks at how the genre of personal fashion blogs and, as an extension to this, the practice of posting self-portraits on social media platforms Twitter, Facebook and Tumblr has enabled women to apparently take control of constructing and exporting feminine identity within the public domain, prioritizing the female (rather than male) gaze. Focusing on the work of three prolific personal fashion bloggers: The Man Repeller (Leandra Medine), Style Bubble (Susie Lau) and The Style Rookie (Tavi Gevinson), Anyan discusses how societal moods of apathy, malaise and boredom have facilitated a need for this generation of women to use social and blogging media to export new versions of the self on a daily basis, and shows that the female respondents are generally highly supportive of the image choices made by the bloggers. This 'safe' discursive space thus serves an implicit need for assurance about personal appearance, with a reaffirmation of conventions of beauty norms and values as explored in Heywood's and Smith's chapters.

This self-referential use of body image is revisited by Anne Burns in Chapter 5 in her analysis of sexualized 'selfies' and how these can be used to produce involuntary pornography, which she explains as being the deliberate creation, publication or distribution of sexualized photographs for the consumption of others, without the subject's consent and/or knowledge. Her analysis of comments that users leave on involuntary porn sites identifies some central assumptions or themes that recur in the discourses surrounding women's 'choice' to engage in private sexualized photography, and draws on Mulvey's notion of the 'male gaze' to explore the traits of 'victim blaming'. These websites embody what Jane (2012) characterizes as a growing prevalence of online hostility, which is not only becoming 'uglier', but also has a number of distinctly gendered characteristics. By examining the degree to which choice is referred to in user comments, Burns considers how the postfeminist rhetoric of individual capability and responsibility is used in this context as a justification for the oppression of women. She shows that these comments work on the assumptions that a woman's decision to participate in naked photography removes her ability to choose whether they are made public, and render her a valid target for the imposition of the choice of others.

In Chapters 6 and 7, the nonconformist female body is explored through a discussion of the comedian Miranda Hart by Rosie White, and then Makiko Iseri looks at the hyper-nonconformist female body as used for commercial gain in Japanese pop culture. As White shows, one of the academic impacts of second wave feminism was the emergence of groundbreaking feminist work on women and television comedy in the 1990s which addressed its potential for subversive, unruly performance, largely focusing on North American stars such as Lucille Ball and Roseanne Arnold (Mellencamp, 1992; Gray, 1994; Rowe, 1995). White's chapter, however, is concerned with how British class identity intersects with the femininity and feminism of a contemporary comedy star and her eponymous sitcom – Miranda Hart and *Miranda* (BBC, 2009–2014). She argues that, if Hart is an 'unruly woman' (Rowe, 1995), she successfully mobilizes discourses of upper middle class Englishness as a means of mitigating the threat of unruly femininity in television comedy, which echoes the argument Smith (Chapter 3) makes about the way in which class and gender interplay in make-over shows such as *What Not To Wear*. In British comedy, class is always in play, and *Miranda* has come under public scrutiny for its 'middle class' constituency (Cook, 1982; Lockyer, 2010; Frost, 2011). *Miranda* and Miranda Hart featured heavily in debates online and in the broadsheet press about class and television comedy, not least because Hart had won three British Comedy Awards in January 2011 (see, for example, Fletcher, 2011; Frost, 2011; Hilton and Ferguson, 2011). Several commentators were keen to stress the 'universal' quality of Hart's comedy (Frost, 2011) or that it 'wasn't about class' (Fletcher, 2011), but there is a complex intersection of class and gender at play in Hart's work. White examines Miranda Hart as a contemporary comedy performer and celebrity, tracing how her television performance and celebrity persona negotiate femininity and feminism through a particular class identity.

The performance of femininity and the unruly body is discussed by Makiko Iseri in Chapter 7. She suggests that, while Japanese subculture – especially what is called '*kawaii* (cute) culture' – currently receives global attention, it has been studied most frequently in the context of Japanese anime/manga or its appropriation by Japanese contemporary artists (Ngai, 2005), and very few readings of *kawaii* highlight another root of this phenomenon: Japanese girls' culture. Iseri investigates the complicated relationship between the particular modes of feminine gender performance in Japanese girls' culture and its politics of bodily flexibility with particular attention to the presentation of the Japanese model, blogger and pop singer Kyary Pamyu Pamyu. Iseri uses the concept of *kawaii* to shed light on the way in which the media images of *kawaii* have been visualized as 'the flexible' in today's socioeconomic context, and asks what is at stake when such non-normative or 'unusual' femininity comes to gain desirable status of 'flexible body'.

Finally, in Chapter 8, Karen Sturgeon-Dodsworth offers an insight into the neo-Victorian texts of the twenty-first century, where the postfeminist discourse of empowerment sits uncomfortably with the female protagonists' roles in film and literature. She explores concepts of female empowerment and agency in twenty-first century neo-Victorian texts and suggests that these are repeatedly betrayed by the re-imposition of a more regressive set of representational strategies. Through a detailed discussion of Guy Ritchie's *Sherlock Holmes* and its recent sequel *Game of Shadows*, Oliver Parker's *Dorian Gray*, Katy Darby's *The Whore's Asylum* and Belinda Starling's *Dora Damage*, she suggests that each is marked by seemingly positive, progressive politics and representations of strong, independent women which are gradually undercut by counter-energies that compromise those progressive politics.

Drawing on Angela McRobbie's (2009) ideas surrounding postfeminist culture, as discussed above in relation to their incorporation into popular culture with the emphasis frequently placed on a vocabulary of 'empowerment', 'freedom' and 'choice', Sturgeon-Dodsworth follows the argument that these offer a faux feminism rather than any real engagement with feminist politics. She suggests that what we witness in the many representations of twenty-first century femininities in neo-Victorian texts as formulated within the seemingly overtly progressive female characters is just such a cultural manifestation: these women at first glance signifying the enlightened nature of the text as they embody and enact independence, agency and choice only for that strength to be effaced. The agency these women initially assert within their respective narratives constitutes a form of appeasement but one that once established is almost immediately compromised and eroded through an insidious imposition of passivity, dependency and domesticity. This process considers that it is in essence the Victorian milieu which serves to legitimize or naturalize that reinforcement of a patriarchal status quo, as progressive contemporary femininities are neutralized and reduced even as they retain the superficial appearance or vestigial trace of an initial progressive strength.

Sturgeon-Dodsworth's chapter finishes this collection of essays by returning to the theme of just how femininity has come to be formed and performed in the twenty-first century. As all the chapters show, the advances made in the law and wider social structures by second wave feminism, and in technology through the development of Web 2.0, have led to a series of 'choices' being made available to women. While the postfeminist context allows for a playfulness with the gaze, these chapters debate just how far this is truly empowering. The underpinning commercial imperatives of female performance, as found in this context throughout these essays, seems to offer an illusion of choice but at the same time prioritizes a formation of femininity that is often curtailing the depth and breadth of such empowerment. The emergence of fourth wave feminists, which sees Web 2.0 being employed as a tool to engage in vibrant and effective campaigning by groups such as @EverydaySexism and @NoMorePage3 but also more local groups, promises a new frontier for feminism in the twenty-first century. Although the democratic space of Twitter and other Web 2.0 sites has left women open to threats and abuse, as Burns discusses in Chapter 5, the law in Britain and other national settings has been used to punish and silence those whose comments are regarded as being the most extreme: in early 2014, two people were jailed in England for abuse and threats made against Caroline Criado-Perez in the case mentioned above. As Higgins and Smith (2014) have shown, the abuse levelled at Criado-Perez was typical of that directed at women in general in that it focused on her appearance and sexuality, and contained threats of sexual violence. Therefore we would suggest that there remains a focus on women's bodies in the twenty-first century, where women feel they are open to debate and need to conform to some ideal, yet at the same time the social and legal changes in society in some ways protect them from the worst excesses. These chapters, then, offer views of twenty-first century feminism in a variety of social and cultural contexts that nevertheless point to only marginal gains in terms of gender equality and can in some cases be seen as being simply a veiled misogyny with underlying traditional discourses of gender division still very much in evidence.

Bibliography

Bates, Laura (2013) 'Shouting back: How women are fighting street harassment', *The Guardian*, 15 January 2013.

Beauvoir, Simone de (1972) *The Second Sex*. London: Jonathan Cape. Translation by M. Ward and R. Howard (first published in French, 1967).

Brooks, Ann (1997) *Postfeminisms: Feminism, Cultural Theory and Cultural Forms*. London: Routledge.

Cook, Jim (ed.) (1982) *BFI Dossier 17: Television Sitcom*. London: British Film Institute.

Coward, Rosalind (1984) *Female Desire: Women's Sexuality Today*. London: Paladin.

Faludi, Susan (1992) *Backlash: The Undeclared War Against Women*. London: Vintage.

Fletcher, Alex (2011) 'Miranda Hart: "*Miranda* is universal, not middle class" ', *Digital Spy*, 27 August 2011. Available online at: http://www.digitalspy.co .uk/tv/news/a337438/miranda-hart-miranda-is-universal-not-middle-class .html#no (accessed 25 September 2013).

Foucault, Michel (1980) *Power/Knowledge: Selected Interviews and Other Writing, 1972–1977*. Brighton: Harvester Wheatsheaf. Translation by C. Gordon et al.

Frost, Vicky (2011) 'TV comedy: Is it really a class issue?', *The Guardian*, 24 January 2011. Available online at: http://www.theguardian.com/tv -and-radio/tvandradioblog/2011/jan/24/tv-comedy-class-miranda-hart (accessed 25 September 2013).

Gallagher, James (3 February 2014) 'Plastic surgery "booming" in the UK', *BBC News*. Available online at: http://www.bbc.co.uk/news/health-25986840 (accessed 3 February 2014).

Genz, Stéphanie (2009) *Postfemininities in Popular Culture*. Basingstoke: Palgrave Macmillan.

Genz, Stéphanie and Benjamin Brabon (2009) *Postfeminism: Cultural Texts and Theories*. Edinburgh: Edinburgh University Press.

Gill, Rosalind (2007) *Gender and the Media*. Cambridge: Polity Press.

Gledhill, Christine (1991) *Stardom: Industry of Desire*. London: Routledge.

Gray, Frances (1994) *Women and Laughter*. Charlottesville: University Press of Virginia.

Higgins, Michael and Angela Smith (2014) 'Disaffiliation and Belonging: Twitter and its Agonisics Publics' *Sociologia e Politiche Sociali*, vol. 17, 2/2014, pp. 77–89.

Hilton, Boyd and Euan Ferguson (2011) 'Are TV sitcoms too middle class?', *The Observer*, 30 January 2011. Available online at: http://www.theguardian .com/commentisfree/2011/jan/30/danny-cohen-middle-class-comedy (accessed 19 November 2013).

Jane, Emma A. (2012) ' "You're a ugly whorish slut" – understanding e-bile', *Feminist Media Studies*, 14(4), pp. 531–546

Lockyer, Sharon (2010) 'Chavs and chav-nots: Social class in *Little Britain*', in Sharon Lockyer (ed.) *Reading Little Britain*. London: I. B. Tauris, pp. 95–110.

Macdonald, Myra (1995) *Representing Women: Myths of Femininity in the Popular Media*. London: Edward Arnold.

McRobbie, Angela (ed.) (1989) *Zoot Suits and Second-Hand Dresses: An Anthology of Fashion and Music*. London: Macmillan.

McRobbie, Angela (2009) *The Aftermath of Feminism: Gender, Culture and Social Change*. London: Sage.

Mellencamp, Patricia (1992) *High Anxiety: Catastrophe, Scandal, Age and Comedy*, Bloomington and Indianapolis: Indiana University Press.

Moseley, Rachel and Jacinda Read (2002) ' "Having it Ally": Popular television (post-) feminism', *Feminist Media Studies*, 2(2), pp. 231–249.

Mulvey, Laura (1975) 'Visual pleasure and narrative cinema', *Screen*, 16(3), pp. 6–18.

Ngai, Sianne (2005) 'The cuteness of the Avant-Garde', *Critical Inquiry*, 31(4), pp. 811–847.

Palmer, Gareth (2004) ' "The New You": Class and transformation in lifestyle television', in Su Holmes and Deborah Jermyn (eds) *Understanding Reality Television*. Routledge: Abingdon pp. 173–190.

Projansky, Sarah (2001) *Watching Rape: Film and Television in Postfeminist Culture*. New York: New York University Press.

Rowe, Kathleen (1995) *The Unruly Woman: Gender and the Genres of Laughter*. Austin: University of Texas Press.

Smith, Angela (2013) 'From girl power to lady power? Postfeminism and *Ladette to Lady*', in Claire Nally and Angela Smith (eds) *Naked Exhibitionism: Gendered Performance and Public Exposure*. London: I. B. Tauris pp. 137–164.

Steele, Valerie (2001) *The Corset: A Cultural History*. New Haven: Yale.

Stacey, Judith (1987) 'Sexism by a subtler name? Postindustrial conditions and postfeminist consciousness in the silicon valley', *Socialist Review*, 96(1987), pp. 7–28

Vermeulen, Timotheus, and va den Akker, Robin(2010) 'Notes on metamodernism', Available online at: http://www.metamodernism.com/ (accessed 20 March 2011).

Whelehan, Imelda (2000) *Overloaded: Popular Culture and the Future of Feminism*. London: The Woman's Press.

Willis, Susan (1990) 'Work(ing) out', *Cultural Studies*, 4(1), pp. 1–18.

2
'Strange Borrowing': Affective Neuroscience, Neoliberalism and the 'Cruelly Optimistic' Gendered Bodies of CrossFit

Leslie Heywood

The history of representation of the female athlete has been cyclic, from the 'babes' and 'muscle molls' of the early twentieth century to the 'hotnesss' quotients assigned in the twenty-first (Heywood and Dworkin, 2000). What has remained fairly consistent is that traditionally feminine athletes are idealized, and more 'masculine' athletes denigrated, with a few notable exceptions in the 1940s, 1990s, and within a specific athletic culture in the present – that of CrossFit, a 10,000-plus global network of affiliated gyms or 'boxes' as they are called within the subculture to mark their back-to-basics, low-tech approach to fitness. CrossFit as a training methodology is a multidisciplinary physical practice where men and women train together in a high-intensity programme run by a coach who takes a small group (anywhere from 5 to 20 people depending on location) through a prescribed set of exercises that includes running, gymnastics, Olympic lifting and powerlifting, rope climbing, tyre flipping, plyometrics, and pretty much anything else that can be imagined. The current representational demographic, though somewhat varied, has become more conservative since the 1990s, but CrossFit marks one emergent cultural site that creates an alternative reality where body expectations and ideals tend to be non-normative, and 'real', functional bodies are idealized. This ideal presents an alternative to the hyperfemininity of athletes idealized in mainstream representations such as those in *ESPN Magazine*. But in its 'maverick' articulations of difference, however, CrossFit can be seen as a characteristic expression of the neoliberal ideology that still undergirds the global economy despite systemic disruptions, critiques and mass protests. These contradictions can only be read within the context of the rhetorics of threat and precarity, and can only be fully explained, I will argue, through an affective neuroscientific perspective that explores conditions of gendered embodiment at the deepest levels. We cannot make sense of the gendered dynamics of CrossFit without examining the ways that these dynamics are structured though the biology of affect as it is shaped by normative social constraints.

Because it does provide a new way of exploring gendered embodiment, cultural ambivalence and contradiction in relation to gender is productively examined within the framework of affect theory. Despite repeated criticism of its biological base, various forms of affective analysis have gained a foothold within the humanities. This 'affective turn' might be articulated best by critical geographer Nigel Thrift: 'distance from biology is no longer seen as a prime marker of social and cultural theory. It has become increasingly evident that the biological constitution of being...has to be taken into account if performative force is ever to be understood, and in particular, the dynamics of birth (and creativity) rather than death.... Human language is no longer assumed to offer the only meaningful model of communication' (Thrift, 2004, p. 59). It is crucial to this formulation that affect occurs prior to cognition: 'The turn to affect is thereby a turn to that "non-reflective" bodily space before thought, cognition and representation – a space of visceral processing' (Papoulias and Callard, 2010, p. 35). Or, as Nicholas Rose puts it, 'No longer are social theories thought progressive by virtue of their distance from the biological. Indeed the reverse assumption is common – it seems that "constructivism" is passé, the linguistic turn has reached a dead end and a rhetoric of materiality is almost obligatory' (Rose, 2013, p. 4). While Thrift's and Rose's words mark a concise summary of the 'affective turn', these assumptions are characterized critically by many in the humanities as 'a prioritization of the biological constitution of being, and of the centrality of affect to understandings of sociality' (Papoulias and Callard, 2010, p. 31). In the critical literature there are at least as many criticisms of affect theory as there are formulations of it, yet it remains vital to contemporary critical readings of culture for reasons I hope to clarify below.

Queer theorist Lauren Berlant provides an affective framework that is particularly useful in analysing the gendered dimensions of contemporary practices of physical culture. In *Cruel Optimism,* Berlant does a sociopolitical analysis of how affect is constructed, deployed and lived in the current historical present of neoliberalism and its aftermath. She defines her concept of 'cruel optimism' in the following terms: 'a relation of cruel optimism exists when something you desire is actually an obstacle to your flourishing' (2010, p. 1). Cruel optimism is a psychological and behavioural response that is a reaction formation – a defence mechanism where anxiety is masked by its opposite – to what Berlant calls the 'genre of crisis' that characterizes our historical present. For Berlant, 'the present moment increasingly imposes itself on consciousness as a moment in extended crisis, with one happening piling on another... an intensified situation in which extensive threats to survival are said to dominate the reproduction of life' (2010, p. 7). Importantly, crisis is a 'genre' because these threats are both real and imagined, actual occurrences (wars, technological malfunctions like the Japan nuclear reactor meltdown and grid failure in the US, climate instability that leads to hurricanes, tsunamis, heatwaves, widespread fires, food and water shortages, global warming, etc.) that in turn fuel a rhetorical sense generated by the 24-hour news cycle. Unlike 'trauma' as an event that has an end, something that occurs and creates chaos until stability returns, the historical present of 'precarity' is 'an ongoing mélange or collection of shattering events' (2010, p. 10) that creates a state in which there is a 'shift in how the older state-liberal-capitalist fantasies shape adjustments to the structural pressures of crisis and loss that are wearing out the power of the good life's traditional fantasy bribe without wearing out the need for a good life' (2010, p. 7). In this way, Berlant's work marks an 'attempt to produce a material context for affect theory' (2010, p. 14).

Berlant's formulation of cruel optimism as a state within which what you desire fulfils on some level but contributes to something more sinister in a larger sense can be applied to a number of historical formations within the present.[1] From the perspective of feminism in the twenty-first century, I would like to focus on the practice of CrossFit – a physical training modality whose hallmark is flexibility and constant variation, the practice of which is said to make each athlete stronger and affectively balanced, 'prepared for anything' – as a particularly gendered version of cruel optimism. On the one hand, CrossFit, has been gender-egalitarian from its inception. Yet because of its cost – usually $120 (USD) per month for coaching and athletic programming within a small group setting – CrossFit performs many other exclusions in terms of who can participate. As such, it seems to provide a space for *some* women that is the antidote to the trivialization of the female body and of the omnipresence of pornographic media images, including those of female athletes, as well as an antidote to fashion images that (still) represent the ectomorphic, impossibly thin (and weak) body as the dominant ideal. Berlant provides a 'material context for affect' that helps us to understand more fully the scrambled articulations of gender in the historical present as they are deployed in physical culture, particularly when her 'material context' is read in conjunction with the particular kind of materiality provided by affective neuroscience.

Insights from neuroscience have become central to understandings of gender and other critical cultural formations. I would argue that a kind of rapprochement between the natural sciences and the humanities is formulable if we look at Berlant's analysis in conjunction with that of affective neuroscientist Jaak Panksepp, whose 'seven affective systems' shared across the brains of all mammals marks the operation of affect at its most basic level. While 'cruel optimism' seems to characterize the manifestations, embodiments and practices of CrossFit's culture in many ways, if we read Berlant's concept in conjunction with Panksepp's affective systems, a different (and more optimistic?) argument might be made about CrossFit's functionality in the historical present.

Reading Berlant and Panksepp in conjunction might provide us with a powerful framework for analysis of gendered embodiment. However, the 'affective turn' my analysis is part of has been criticized by many theorists in the humanities. By using Berlant and affective neuroscience in dialogue in this way, I might be performing the kind of characteristic misstep Papoulias and Callard outline in the following terms:

> While neuroscience frames the affective as part of a system of regulation that makes both self and social coherence possible, in cultural theory's narratives, by contrast, affectivity becomes a placeholder for the inherent dynamism and mutability of matter.

[Our] article interrogates the consequences of cultural theory's strange borrowings from neuroscience and developmental psychology in their institution of a model of subjectivity preoccupied with a lived present in excess of the hold of habit and embodied history.

(2010, p. 30)

Although I might be seen to be guilty of precisely this kind of 'strange borrowing', I would argue that situating affective neuroscience in relation to Berlant doesn't situate an analysis of experience 'in excess of the hold and habit of embodied history' but precisely an explication of the specific interaction effects between neuroscience's affective 'systems of regulation' and critical affective theory's 'inherent dynamism and mutability of matter'. I will argue that the opposition constructed here – determinate, fixed systems on the part of neuroscience and completely open-ended mutability on the part of critical affect theory in the humanities – is a false one, and that Jaak Panksepp's and Stephen Porges's work in particular articulates a two-way model where each pole produces and affects the other.

Panksepp's and Porges's affective neuroscience: Cross-species affect in the autonomic nervous system and the mammalian brain

A central research question in gender studies has been how gender becomes embodied – how cultural stereotypes become literally imbricated in the flesh, affecting how we move, talk or even perceive. But the mechanisms by which this embodiment occurs have remained mysterious. The most recent advances in affective neuroscience, a field founded by Jaak Panksepp and based on four decades of empirical research, help us to begin mapping the embodiment of gender as an affective experience that occurs in response to environmental cues of safety. Panksepp categorizes affect in terms of the brain's 'primary process affective systems', and makes a convincing argument for a 'bottom up' model – one that articulates the indissociable relation between affect and cognition, emotion and reason, biology and culture, the brain and the mind. As affective neuroscience has spelled out in some detail in its theories of 'functional connectivity', none of these binaries is possible without the other (Cromwell and

Panksepp, 2011, pp. 20–31). When critical theorist Ruth Leys claims that in affect theory 'what I feel is just a matter of my physiological condition' (2011, p. 455), this is a fundamental misunderstanding of affective neuroscientific models. Instead, in Panksepp's work, 'brain-behavior processes' are the products of interaction effects between each, neural circuits that include the control functions of the primary process emotional states themselves: 'more realistic models that incorporate dynamic properties and bidirectional interactive multi-way communications' (2011, p. 2031). Instead of occurring through a top-down hierarchy in which cognition occurs first and is the controlling mechanism, neural activity has been shown to occur bidirectionally in multiple regions. According to Panksepp, 'lower BrainMind functions are embedded and re-represented in higher brain functions, which yield not only traditional bottom-up controls but also top-down regulations of emotionality. This provides two-way avenues of control that can be seen to be forms of "circular causality" that respect the brain as a fully integrated organ' (Panksepp and Biven, 2012, p. 77). As such, 'our higher (neocortical) mental functions can create art and madness out of our emotions, but they cannot generate feelings *on their own'* (*Archaeology* 81, emphasis in original). It is fundamental to Panksepp's work that affect precedes cognition, but cognition in turn shapes affect in a bidirectional feedback loop.

Panksepp identifies seven core emotional systems that provide a neurobiology of affect: SEEKING, RAGE, FEAR, LUST, CARE, PANIC and PLAY (1998). The systems most relevant to affect in sport are SEEKING, RAGE and PLAY. The SEEKING system is the appetitive motivational system that 'energizes engagement with the world as individuals seek goods from the environment as well as meaning in everyday life' (2009, p. 9), and is a generalized substrate for all other emotional processes. The PLAY system provides a safe context for young (human and non-human) animals to learn what they can or cannot do to each other. It can provide a physical engagement with others that is experienced as joyous, with therapeutic indications for adults, whose play urges can be re-energized by bodily activities such as dance or sport (Panksepp, 2009). The neocortex is not needed for this system, as it isn't for the others, but the PLAY system has effects on the cortex, programming it to be fully social (1998, 2000). In this sense, a very important function of sport is to programme the brain to be social. Both the PLAY and SEEKING systems are activated in a context of safety.[2]

The third core emotional system most relevant to physical practice is the RAGE system, whose expression can be linked to feelings of empowerment and assertion-activation based in a perception (real or imagined) of threat in an organism's environment. The RAGE system is activated in response to threat, and evolutionarily speaking, being held immobile as prey (Panksepp, 2000). CARE is crucial to social engagement and learned empathy, and FEAR, based on an interpretation of threat to survival, precipitates RAGE or PANIC/GRIEF.

These systems, Panksepp writes, 'suggest nested-hierarchies of BrainMind affective processing, with primal emotional functions being foundational for secondary-process learning and memory mechanisms, which interface with tertiary-process cognitive-thoughtful functions of the BrainMind' ('Cross-Species Affective Neuroscience Decoding,' Panksepp, 2000). Panksepp's work, then, has established the basis for emotional continuities across species, and for a bidirectional, interactional theory of mind that links affect and cognition even as these processes are seen to proceed from different parts of the brain. Panksepp's seven affective systems represent one of the first levels of response to stimuli.

These levels of response, I will argue, contribute to the ways gender becomes internalized and performed. Our most basic motivations are affectively based, and one of our deepest affective needs is for a sense of safety, for without it no social engagement is possible. Since a sense of safety is contextually determined, provided by the cues and responses of those in one's immediate environment, the gender codes present in that environment cue the individual in terms of what they may and may not do to remain safe within the group. This is the same in terms of all kinds of positional cues, from those related to gender and sexuality to those related to race, social standing or any other indices of social engagement. Contextual cues related to gender and other variables affect us at the very deepest levels of embodiment, from the viscera to the brainstem to the prefrontal cortex, modulating our perception, responses and behaviours.

Behavioural neuroscientist Stephen Porges provides a link between the primary process affects located in the brainstem that Panksepp analyses and the neurological responses of the autonomic nervous system and core viscera such as the heart and lungs. Porges's Polyvagal Theory articulates a level of affective response to stimuli that is an elaboration on Panksepp's seven primary process systems. While Panksepp's work lets us understand neural circuits between higher brain structures and those in the brainstem, Porges's work allows us to understand the neural circuits between the brainstem and visceral organs: 'neural circuits mediating the reciprocal communication between body states and brainstem structures, which impact on the availability of these affective circuits' (2011, p. 258).

The main postulates of the Polyvagal Theory are that emotional regulation and social behaviour are psychological processes that respond to events, environment and people. They shape our sense of self, help form relationships, and determine whether we feel safe in various contexts. Neural circuits are bidirectional, biobehavioural processes that mediate reciprocal communication between body states and brainstem structures: psychological processes influence body states, and body states influence psychological processes like perception (2011, pp. 257, 259). Polyvagal Theory provides the context for cognition – the bodily states it describes make cognition possible or impossible. In it, neuroception – the unconscious perception of safety – triggers a response according to these systems, starting with the social engagement system, progressing to 'fight/flight' response if threat is perceived, and ending with the 'freeze' behaviours as a last resort. It precedes perception. Therefore the phylogenetic stage of the autonomic nervous system informs the behavioural, physiological and affective features of reactivity to things in the environment. Physiological state limits the range of adaptive behaviours and psychological experiences (2011, p. 265). Trauma can limit an individual's ability to engage the vagal brake and decreased heart rate necessary for the operation of the social engagement system because trauma victims often have faulty neuroception and become hypervigilant, always reacting to the environment or people as though they were a threat. Adequate functioning of the social engagement system is particularly important since it helps detect and express signals of safety in the environment – it 'distinguish[es] and emit[s] facial expressions and intonation of vocalizations.... By calming the viscera and regulating facial muscles, this system enables and promotes positive social interactions in safe contexts' (2011, p. 270). In other words, the social engagement system helps us read body language, which is what dogs do as their primary modality of communication, and which is what we do when we are using our pre-conscious neuroception.

One of the main implications of Panksepp's and Porges's work for theories of gendered embodiment is that even if affect triggers other processes, it is informed and shaped by the secondary- and tertiary-process memory and cultural learning. Gender is articulated at the level of the social context that provides cues of safety and belonging or cues of threat. Here biology becomes culture, and culture becomes biology. It is at the deepest levels of affect that such cues are internalized, regulated or rejected. Since the history of reaction to female athletes in the public sphere – and the unsettling of gender they represent – has been complicated and ambivalent, it will be useful to my analysis to try to pin down the contradictions of our current cultural moment in order to show how gender is still operational in and through female athletes at the affective levels Panksepp and Porges have mapped.

The rhetoric of gender: Naked athletes in *ESPN Magazine*

Based on this kind of affective analysis, what then might an embodied affective reaction to gendered media images – in this case, images of athletes – look like? What affects are mobilized and instantiated when one views, say, *ESPN Magazine*'s *Body Issue*?' Cultural cues and bodily affects can be seen to interact in the process Berlant outlines:

> All attachment is optimistic, if we describe optimism as the force that moves you out of yourself and into the world in order to bring closer the satisfying *something* that you cannot generate on your own but sense in the wake of a person, a way of life, an object, project, concept, or scene ... whatever the *experience* of optimism ... the *affective structure* of an optimistic attachment involves a sustaining inclination to return to the scene of fantasy that enables you to expect that *this* time, nearness to *this* thing will help you or a world to become different in just the right way.
>
> (2010, pp. 1–2)

Like Panksepp's SEEKING system, the function of which is to, precisely, 'move you out of yourself', affective structures always operate

in relation to everything around them, a basic motivational engagement to interact with and negotiate whatever environmental conditions one finds. The current social context in the Western world
is one in which one experiences the diminishment of what Berlant
calls the rhetoric of 'the good life' and one's ability to access it.
Given this particular structure of our historical present, feminism and
other forms of critical theory must be framed within what Berlant
terms the 'contemporary world of spreading precarity and normative
dissolution' (2010, p. 13). Feminism's earlier historical forms, all taking place within a rights-based framework, presupposed 'concepts of
autonomy, agency and freedom – the central terms by which subjectivity has been understood in the twentieth century and beyond
[and that] ha[s] been central to feminist politics', and these concepts are increasingly untenable in current conditions (Grosz, 2010,
p. 139). Instead, Berlant's 'precarity framework' might be seen as a
background for mainstream iconography, and this framework makes
'autonomy, agency, and freedom' residual concepts whose continuing presence interacts with 'spreading precarity'. If we read those
conditions in conjunction with Panksepp and Porges, we have a
situation where the underlying nervous system in many individuals is one attuned to threat, and therefore invoking the fight/flight
response rather than the social engagement system. Even in First
World conditions, we experience ourselves as under threat and
have become, dispositionally speaking, 'thin-skinned', our defences
stripped by information overload, subject to a precarity rhetoric for
as long as we engage with our electronics, and in some cases, subject
to precarity's manifestations.

A major part of the engagement with our environments is an
engagement with images, and in terms of athletics, the visual horizon can be no better represented than through the yearly *Body Issue*
published by *ESPN Magazine*. According to Mike Chiari, writing for
The Bleacher Report, '*ESPN The Magazine's: The Body Issue* is one of
the most highly anticipated magazine issues to hit newsstands....
With male and female stars from a variety of different sports and
backgrounds posing in the buff, it is truly a unique presentation.
While well-known athletes... are the main draws, lesser-known athletes stand to gain legions of new fans' (bleacherreport.com). Because
athletic bodies, as the ESPN tagline goes, are now considered in mainstream iconography to be the 'Bodies We Want' – ostensibly those we

want to look like, and couple with – the *Body Issue* gives us a place to focus on contemporary deployments of gender in a mass context. Because the gendered bodies I consider might appear at first glance to be posed in visually similar ways since they are all naked, I will examine gender in two specific images constructed to resemble each other, that of Polish tennis player Agnieszka Radwanska, and the other of San Francisco 49ers quarterback Colin Kaepernick.

In these images, a similar positioning of the bodies, and the nudity of each, belies a gendered difference in representation. Despite the similar positioning of the bodies, and despite the fact that even in a visual horizon in which our most high-achieving, culturally respected men are objectified too – constructed as eye-candy, boy-toys, in terms of their physical 'hotness' – there is something different about the solidity of the male body's gendered flesh, in this image. Light and shadow is used to make Kaepernick appear more than sexualized, more than sex, more than flesh. While Radwanska's image is bathed in light, Kaepernick's is surrounded by dark, light only used to strategically highlight the side of his face, the top of his shoulder, and the powerful line from his shoulder to spine, buttock and hamstring. He is lying on his stomach, completely nude except for his full upper-body tattoos, on a long black leather sofa. His torso is propped up on his elbows, a tattoo in capital letters spelling 'RESPECT' running the length of the muscular arm that is turned toward the camera.

The image is constructed in such a way that 'respect' is what the image invokes in the viewer. Kaepernick appears as a composite of sinews and cables, a gleam of tattooed muscle almost panther-like in the way the shoulder curves to the hip, a flesh so dense it seems to be composed of marble. He could be a statue if not for the intensity of his gaze, his eyes boring directly into the viewer in a way that invokes a presence formidably alive. Shot at eye-level, so that you see his body straight on from the side, what you see is not sexuality, approachability, but a sleek S-curve of muscle from shoulder to side buttock – this is a body built to perform powerful feats, and the person who will perform them is brought to the fore. Instead of smiling at the viewer, inviting them in, Kaepernick's chin is tilted down so that his mouth is hidden behind his powerful biceps, suggesting little accessibility but rather a form that should provoke awe and a sense of danger. This is a body built for power, built for speed, informed by a wilful, powerful subjectivity, and we are meant to experience it as such.

By contrast, in the Radwanska photo, she is floating in a pool on a blue plastic raft, the tennis balls bobbing in the water all around her the only thing signalling that this is an athlete we are looking at. Instead of dark, dangerous and dense, everything is frothy and light, superficial, the slenderness of Radwanska's limbs – long legs and arms with little visible muscle – the morphological counterpart to the plastic float she rests on, her body insubstantial and conventionally thin. The angle of the shots reinforces this. Radwanska is shot from above, making her appear smaller and emphasizing her nakedness (exposed butt crack) and situating her so that the viewer is literally looking down at her. Light dances on the water and she floats, smiling in the stereotypically feminine 'come hither' way, corner of her mouth turned up, head tilted slightly, inviting access. There is no muscular potentiality in her narrowed down limbs: she signifies as conventionally feminine – pretty, frothy, made for fun rather than as athletic, powerful or self-determined. The difference in the images is striking. One clearly marks a self-determined intentionality and an athlete's body that invokes a powerful presence, while the other fails to signify as athletic at all, instead emphasizing sexual access, weakness and vulnerability. It is notable that this image makes Radwanska's arms and legs appear so thin and fragile, when in competition shots she looks much more powerful. Some codes seem to persevere despite female athletes' successes: weakness, vulnerability, sexual accessibility.

Standard racialized codes persevere in these images as well: Kaepernick's racially hybrid body is constructed partly as dangerous, animalistic, fierce, while Radwanska's white body is non-threatening. The juxtaposition of images reveals how race and gender often intertwine in visual iconography to produce a complex blend of associations and codes: feminine equals insubstantial and white, darker masculine equals a visceral potential animality and power (it is important that most of the shots of completely white male athletes in the *ESPN Body Issues* show them in a sardonic pose, acting and covering their genitals all in good fun as if they always retain a distance from their bodies that racialized male bodies do not). In the juxtaposition of these images, we see the reinforcement of racial and gender stereotypes long in circulation brought into the historical present where all bodies form a kind of currency.

Why do such representations matter – how might a viewer's *affective* response be structured in response to them if we combine

Berlant's analysis of the contemporary 'genre of crisis' with Panksepp's and Porges's delineations of the sub-cortical affective systems in the brain, and the autonomic nervous response we see in Polyvagal Theory? Recall that in Porges and Panksepp we see a bidirectional circuit moving from a neuroception of the image (the individual's interpretation of that image according to safety cues) and resulting response of social engagement, fight/flight or freeze. From there nervous response engages Panksepp's seven affective systems, stimulating one or more to produce a response that then engages with mechanisms important to secondary-process learning, which is where memories of experience with gender and memories of cultural codes come into play. From there tertiary-process cognitions inform response, with the prefrontal cortex functioning to interpret the images at a conscious level. These in turn inform top-down cognitive regulations and conditioned responses, which shift back down to the primary process affects found in Panksepp's systems and Porges's levels of vagal response (Figure 2.1).

Given this physiological process, informed as it is by all kinds of cultural experiences, codes and meanings, an individual with a

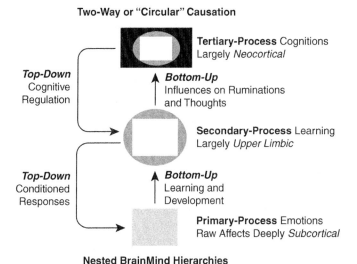

Two-Way or "Circular" Causation

Tertiary-Process Cognitions
Largely *Neocortical*

Top-Down Cognitive Regulation

Bottom-Up Influences on Ruminations and Thoughts

Secondary-Process Learning
Largely *Upper Limbic*

Top-Down Conditioned Responses

Bottom-Up Learning and Development

Primary-Process Emotions
Raw Affects Deeply *Subcortical*

Nested BrainMind Hierarchies

Figure 2.1 Panksepp, *The Archaeology of Mind*, p. 78

'queered' sensibility of gender might find the normative images represented by Kaepernick and Radwanska distressing or even threatening, so that, say, a flight response at the level of the vagus nerve would then trigger Panksepp's PANIC/FEAR system, which in turn might react with multiple memories of negative experiences related to the cultural enforcement of gender norms, which might then be interpreted at the cognitive level as 'the world is one that is different from and hostile to me', which would in turn cause a dampening of the SEEKING system and the social engagement system, resulting in depression or lack of motivation for engaging with the world. There is a need for work that specifically maps the trajectory from the most basic forms of affective response to cultural cues related to gender and other variables. The disciplinary segregation that has until this point kept biological approaches such as affective neuroscience distinct from and in opposition to cultural approaches like gender studies has been detrimental to progress in either field, but now the stage has been set for research that shows how gender is deployed in ways that effect and shape embodiment and experience at the deepest levels.

Gendering CrossFit: Alternatives and rearticulations

The cultural context of 'precarity' and perpetual threat, the trauma that has ceased to be traumatic through repetition, is also a context underwritten in the visual realm by athletic bodies in both conventional and transgressive codes. Visual representations are a vital part of the environment to which subjects react. If we respond at the deepest level to threat through an autonomic neuroception that tells us we are not safe, we may, according to our racial, sexual, gendered and class-based positionalities, do any number of things to make ourselves feel more safe. Physical practices, then, might be seen to offer a way out of precarity, a way to build oneself into something substantial, to be 'prepared for anything'. The remedy that is also a poison, a 'cruel optimism' in which the fulfilment of your desires also destroys you, as a 'remedy' for gender and the ways conventional conceptualizations are mapped through the mass media, CrossFit (and other forms of athletic activity) both gives and takes away. If CrossFit is one response to the historically present state of precarity, it can be important to track the ways in which participating in CrossFit might help 'cure' disparaging gender codes, but might also undermine the person practising them, since their participation also embeds them in a network of consumer practices that are distinctly part of economic neoliberalism and all its attendant problems. How does CrossFit, then, 'cure', and how does it 'harm'?[3]

Like Berlant, cultural critic Kelly Moore also addresses the 'historical present' of gendered bodily practices in terms of their articulation through the global formation of neoliberalism. In her article, 'Fear and fun: Science and gender, emotion and embodiment under neoliberalism,' she claims that 'emotion-worlds attached to the political economy have patterns that encourage citizens to normalize extant arrangements', and she goes on to analyse what she calls 'the emotion-world of women's "exercise" since the 1980s' (2013). That emotional world now belongs to what she terms the 'striver class' – which 'includes what were formerly known as the working-to-middle classes, but who are now reconfigured and defined by their mobility aspirations...losers stand still'. Mobility is embodied in the assumption behind exercise that 'morphology and all other features of the self are malleable and can be changed through calculative practices that join together in the body and the mind'. Bodywork is 'flexible' and infinitely varied, and exercise discourses are full of advice to 'never stick to one thing' so as to avoid boredom. Such body work is 'expected to be joyful...the labor of producing a body is turned into "fun."' Moore captures the open-endedness and process-oriented temporality of current physical practice, where goals are present but ever-receding, infinitely deferred, when she describes a 'web of embodied women at work-play, endlessly producing but never reaching a goal...the consumer-entrepreneur who is always reinvesting, seeking forms of satisfaction, looking for opportunities' (2013). While Moore focuses on specifically women's exercise practices such as Zumba, Hoopnotica, and various forms of yoga and Pilates, I will examine CrossFit as a mixed-gender activity that, because it presumes men and women can and should do the same physical training, seems to undermine gender assumptions and create a more gender egalitarian space. While it does do this to some extent, and to that extent provides a means to fulfil women's desires for achievement, strength and respect within their communities, as a form of Berlant's 'cruel optimism' and as a manifestation of postfeminist critique, CrossFit simultaneously undermines that fulfilment through its enthusiastic participation in the neoliberal dictates of 'flexibility', 'constant variation', continual work and 'fun', the work of self-production that never stops, and that measures the individual in relation to an extrinsic, arbitrarily constructed sets of values rather than an intrinsic sense of value.

Not coincidentally, 'flexibility' and 'fun' are two CrossFit cornerstones. Because CrossFit is a programme that is reliant on continuous variation of exercises and repetitions schemes, it is a 'general preparedness' kind of training of camaraderie and back-to-the-playground mentality (movements include things like jump roping, rope climbing, box jumping and monkey bars swinging, which most people haven't done since childhood). Characteristic of the historical present in that it articulates a rhetoric of safety and flexibility simultaneously – it is said to provide physical preparedness for anything, and the ability to meet the needs of any situation – CrossFit is, perhaps, the ideal neoliberal body practice. According to its founder, Greg Glassman (a former gymnast and son of a Hughes Aircraft rocket scientist), CrossFit is:

> the principal strength and conditioning program for many police academies and tactical operations teams, military special operations units, champion martial artists, and hundreds of other elite and professional athletes worldwide. Our program delivers a fitness that is, by design, broad, general, and inclusive. Our specialty is not specializing. Combat, survival, many sports, and life reward this kind of fitness and, on average, punish the specialist. The CrossFit program is designed for universal scalability making it the perfect application for any committed individual... We've used our same routines for elderly individuals with heart disease and cage fighters one month out from televised bouts. We scale load and intensity; we don't change programs. The needs of Olympic athletes and our grandparents differ by degree not kind. Our terrorist hunters, skiers, mountain bike riders and housewives have found their best fitness from the same regimen. Thousands of athletes worldwide have followed our workouts posted daily on this site and distinguished themselves in combat, the streets, the ring, stadiums, gyms and homes.
>
> (crossfit.com)

It is not insignificant that in CrossFit rhetoric, 'combat, streets, gyms, and homes' are all represented at the same level. 'Streets and homes', in the context of 'combat', precisely define Berlant's culture of precarity, where these levels of experience are conflated and one uses one's sports training to prepare for survival in a neuroceptive sense – the sense that even before perception, 'the world is threatening, therefore I must be prepared'. It is instructive that CrossFit wants to '*punish* the specialist', as if it were a punitive fitness modality meant to establish its efficacy at all costs, to annihilate the opposition in no uncertain terms.

CrossFit articulates an unapologetically oppositional stance to the mainstream fitness industry (whose models have not fully caught up to the dynamism of the current global economy), and is fully in alignment with the larger context of neoliberalism. Glassman calls himself a 'rabid libertarian', and asserts that this philosophy – one possible manifestation of neoliberalism – reflects CrossFit (Glassman YouTube). This is perhaps one of the reasons why people outside the CrossFit movement often refer to it as a 'cult' – CrossFit culture takes itself very seriously, seeing itself as doing nothing less than facilitating its participants' survival, training them to be ever-vigilant, engaged in constant self-improvement in terms of that survivability. Within CrossFit culture, being supportive of each other within the confines of the group is an absolute cornerstone – anyone who isn't supportive is reprimanded or shunned – which helps to create an atmosphere of group bonding, a sense of 'us' against the world that tends to make CrossFit practitioners fanatically devoted to both CrossFit and to the community within their own CrossFit gym.

In the perpetual 'genre of crisis' that Berlant outlined, the cultural atmosphere of precarity that necessarily triggers an individual's neurologically based neuroceptions (perceptions of threat) and attendant stress responses, CrossFit offers the perfect affective response or 'affective balancing' – at a price – to those who can afford it.[4] At the physiological level, after participating in the high intensity interval and strength training for the day, which is very taxing, the combination of fatigue and anti-stress hormones released causes Porges's vagal brake to come into operation, keeping the heart rate down and making the individual less reactive to anything in his/her environment and more open to social engagement. CrossFit also provides an environment for the activation of Panksepp's PLAY system, which leads to a physical engagement with others that is experienced as joyous, a self-assertion that is practised in a context within which one feels emotionally supported and safe. The fulfilment of hard training done within a supportive group environment may also be conducive to the release of the 'bonding hormone' oxytocin, which Porges claims interacts with the vagal brake and its reduction of heart rate to further create positive conditions for deployment of the social engagement system.

All of these are positive manifestations and experiences. Yet if CrossFit seems to provide a safe environment where individual efforts are supported by the group, it is also directly in alignment with neoliberal principles of deregulation and non-interference. It is a physical practice in which flexibility and variation are deployed in service of larger norms, the individual forged through an intense and infinitely ongoing encounter with obstacles – the 'WOD' (workout of the day, whatever that happens to be) from which one emerges victorious each time. From a gendered perspective, part of its opposi-tional, maverick status is related to its ideals of functional movement and increased performance, from which emerge CrossFit's own visual iconography and body ideals. Initially, from a gender perspective these might be seen as progressive, a rewriting of beauty ideals from weakness to strength.

'Strong is the new beautiful' or 'strong is the new skinny' are fre-quently invoked statements and images that make the rounds of the CrossFit community social networks. If mainstream athletic iconog-raphy like that in *ESPN Magazine's Body Issue* previously analysed contributes to a cultural horizon of threat for anyone who is gender counter-normative, CrossFit might seem to offer an alternative. This CrossFit blogger articulates an often-repeated set of claims within the CrossFit community when he writes that

> Individuals who participate in CrossFit usually develop muscu-lar and toned bodies. Because fitness and athleticism are being encouraged, women are able to unlock the potential behind their bodies. Women are also able to see how strong they are capable of being. Previously many people assumed women were signif-icantly weaker than men. Because of all the new media about fitness, woman are able to fully commit to CrossFit and embrace the lifestyle that comes with it. While I was working out at the

CrossFit gym this past summer, I got to witness the motivation and dedication that women had. They were motivated to develop their bodies and build muscle. A lot of women used to fear becoming bulky or too muscular. Now that there are beautiful women advertising their muscles, more women are comfortable with becoming strong. They look forward to sculpting their bodies and living a healthy lifestyle.

(http://r23nikita.blogspot.com/2012/10/
strong-is-new-bautiful.html)

If this blogger now sees women who are 'motivated to develop their bodies and build muscle', in CrossFit, it must be mentioned that we have been here before, and to little appreciable gain. Much like the advent of strong women bodybuilders in the 1980s and 1990s, of whom I have written extensively elsewhere, the assumptions articulated here reflect those of the larger CrossFit community (see Heywood, 1998). CrossFit constructs itself as rebellious, as a departure from dominant forms of exercise (two main CrossFit suppliers named themselves 'Rogue' and 'Maverick', and this is repeated in the names of many CrossFit gyms) and continues that rebellion through its acceptance and encouragement of strong women. Therefore the CrossFit beauty ideal is one that is deliberately oppositional to dominant norms of the skinny body. Women are 'rogue' in this culture, are 'maverick', much like CrossFit culture more generally – except the 'maverick' nature of this morphological, affective articulation operates precisely within the neoliberal norms of flexibility, constant reinvestment and self-reinvention.

The neoliberal sense of the gender 'maverick' is captured in a popular video made by CrossFit headquarters and often shared on YouTube, called 'Beauty in Strength' (https://www.youtube.com/watch?v=5zvqNHDTf8Y). The video articulates precisely the 'cruel optimism' of the historical present – women who see themselves as defying gender norms – using CrossFit – as a way of being strong, present, self-determined. These are precisely all the ideals the context of neoliberalism has concurrently undermined in the sense that there are now less opportunities, less of a social safety net, even as self-determination is encouraged. 'CrossFit giveth and it taketh away' – an articulation of a 'cruel optimism' that seems to confer the very thing that its participation in the global economy facilitates, one could not have a clearer manifestation and articulation of neoliberalism than the 'maverick' nature expressed by participants in CrossFit – particularly women. 'CrossFit has made me more confident, stronger, more fit than I've ever been … I'm not working out to look good, I'm working out to be strong, to be fit' one of the subjects in the video states. The women all talk about how men now find muscles beautiful in women, and how they want muscles themselves, and how 'women have changed with CrossFit'.

Similarly, the 'butt test', which became a meme in 2012, articulates an ideal based on the body's functionality rather than its looks. The 'butt test' measures the size of the gluteus maximus, and those that 'passed' had butts big enough to stop, if they were lying face down on the floor, a weightlifting bar loaded with large weight plates. A video released by CrossFit of some of the best female CrossFit athletes became viral, and those women who passed the test were lauded, and those who failed prescribed more squats (https://www.youtube.com/watch?v=4_ymRxOqo8U).

It is affectively inspiring to see these women exhorting each other towards strength and muscular development. It makes one want to join the community of like-minded gender-freaks, to partake in the alternatives seemingly offered here. Here, what was previously positioned as a beauty ideal, a small butt, is represented instead as something that needs to be remedied, changed – the woman who doesn't pass the 'butt test' needs to do more squats, have a bigger butt, because if she does so she will be able to handle more weight. 'The butt test' creates a new ideal to work for that seems to be 'maverick' in its deployment of gender codes, and that finally equates beauty with function. But this rhetoric of hope and 'change' takes place within a larger framework where opportunities for such 'change' are not offered to all, or even many, and those changes are contained by the very structure that sustains them in the first place. CrossFit athletes continually work on their bodies towards an ever-changing, ever-receding set of goals so that the work itself becomes the point, and the CrossFit lifestyle, with all its attendant economic mechanisms, perpetuates itself indefinitely into the future.

Reading affective neuroscience in conjunction with the larger cultural context of precarity rhetorics interlaced with the neoliberal exhortations to individual achievement, the SEEKING system universal to all mammals leads us to engage with a historical present of precarity that is inimical to our being, that cannot help but trigger the neuroception of threat, helps us understand why CrossFit has become such a widespread phenomenon in the privileged sectors that can afford it. The neuroception of precarity sets off a cascade of responses that make us particularly susceptible to neoliberal ideologies of self-determination and survival independent of outside help. CrossFit manipulates these biocultural, physiological responses so precisely, and these responses so characterize people's experience of the historical present, that CrossFit's affiliate network has grown from 3000 affiliates worldwide to more than 7000 in *a single year*. Glassman's sensibility is so much of the moment that older gyms, locked in a model of self-improvement in response to particular cultural ideals (rather than to survival in response to flexible circumstance) cannot hope to provide fitness practices that speak to the particular set of historical conjunctions that motivates CrossFitters at the affective level, or that fills all the affective needs CrossFit addresses (http://map.crossfit.com/).

Historically excluded from its purview, women are perhaps particularly affectively susceptible to the rhetoric of self-determination (see Heywood, 2007). While CrossFit's exhortations against ego are more inclusive towards women than are the dynamics of traditional sports, that 'inclusivity' isn't blameless. 'Go about improving yourself' – indefinitely – is what CrossFit exhorts the individual to do. CrossFit provides a space of inclusion, where, if you can afford it, you can belong to the group that is 'forging elite fitness' (the marketing slogan CrossFit used until its partnership with Reebok), and accumulate PRs (Personal Records) that testify to your change and your growing strength – whether you are man or woman, old or young.[5] Yet CrossFit's ultimate function, the remaking of the individual along the norms of the neoliberal consumer economy, the participation of the individual in the endless project of self-making, marks an inclusion in a very normative project rather than a 'maverick' one (www.forbes.com).

CrossFit is undoubtedly a contemporary manifestation of 'cruel optimism'. It is a unique medicine, a *pharmakon* that, perhaps especially for women who would like to articulate themselves in terms of non-normative gender ideals, seems to offer a 'cure' for the banality of ubiquitous images of femininity, a real environment where one's physical strength is supported, idealized, even honoured. CrossFit seems to offer a supportive community in the global context of the dissolution of community, *but it also promotes the survival of the few,* those with money and leisure time enough to make CrossFit a part of their daily lives. CrossFit is a 'body project' that is a reaction formation in response to neuroceptions of precarity, a precarity that is undergirded by both neoliberal rhetoric and practice. But CrossFit is also a mechanism for 'affective balance' in response to precarity, a system of physical training that physiologically regulates stress responses in a way that makes daily life more negotiable, enjoyable, possible – even, so to speak, more *optimistic*. On the physiological level, it helps restore affective balance on a daily basis. CrossFit, provides a space for practitioners of 'cruel optimism', who choose it as an antidote to systemic conditions of precarity. CrossFit is especially 'cruelly optimistic' in a gendered sense, for it offers a way out of limiting old ideas of female physical incompetence and weakness through a neoliberal practice that might provide gender solidarity to an in-group that can afford it, but that limits these gender transgressions to the economic demands of its subculture.

Notes

1. Berlant's conception of cruel optimism is informed by a long critical history that extends back through the early poststructuralism of Deleuze and Guattari, Foucault and Derrida, and from Derrida to Plato. In his introduction to Deleuze and Guattari's critical 1972 opus *Anti-Oedipus*, Foucault writes of 'the fascism in us all, in our heads and in our everyday behavior, the fascism that causes us to love power, to desire the very thing that dominates and exploits us' (Foucault in Deleuze and Guattari, 1977, p. xiii). A different version of the same idea was developed by Derrida in his reading of Plato's concept of the *pharmakon*, the remedy that is also a poison, the cure that destroys. In Derrida's reading of Plato's *Phaedrus*, he analyses writing as a 'remedy' that can help memory, but can also inhibit it since in time one remembers the writing rather than the original thing that is supposed to be remembered. 'There is no such thing as a harmless remedy. The *pharmakon* can never be simply beneficial' (Derrida, 1981, p. 99). In order to fully analyse the contradictions of women's body ideals as they are scrambled through representational horizons and practices, we need the lens of the *'pharmakon'* and its most historically recent articulation in Berlant's 'cruel optimism'.
2. The stimulation of the PLAY system and the way that stimulation can rebalance affect is central to what Panksepp calls Affective Balance Therapy, which is accomplished through play as 'bodily vigor, spontaneity, and

creativeness of real, physical play ... Psychiatric distress can be conceptualized as overturned tables that need to be set right, and there is unlikely to be any stronger emotional aid than that contained in the joyous potentials of PLAY' (2009, p. 21).

3. I should acknowledge that, through my own participation in CrossFit, I am a devoted practitioner of 'cruel optimism'. I hold multiple CrossFit trainer certifications, train five days a week using CrossFit methodology, and own a CrossFit box.

4. Because CrossFit is based on a coaching model where athletes come to a small class whose programme is written by certified coaches and whose movements are supervised by a coach or coaches each day, it is an intensive, hands-on model created in opposition to the anonymous pay-your-cash-and-you're-on-your-own model of the regular gyms. The scale is much smaller – a given 'box' (the name for CrossFit gyms, which indicates CrossFit's back-to-basics nature) can only serve a limited number of athletes. One pays for this kind of personal attention: instead of a typical $200 per year gym membership, many CrossFit boxes charge around $200 per month. The cost does seem to have an impact on CrossFit's characteristic demographic, which is largely white men and women making more than $100,000 per year. See, for instance, http://www.jonathonmcmahon.com/1/post/2013/06/the-demographics-of-a-crossfit-box.html.

5. After functioning for years on its own largely through its website and affiliate network, CrossFit the corporation formed a partnership with Reebok, which now uses the CrossFit name to sell a line of specially designed apparel and shoes for CrossFit athletes, and which sponsors the annual CrossFit Games – a global competition that pits the best CrossFit athletes against each other in a three-day series of gruelling events and currently awards $275,000 for the winner of the individual men's and women's competitions.

Bibliography

Berlant, Lauren (2010) *Cruel Optimism*. Durham: Duke UP. Available online at: http://bleacherreport.com/articles/1699882-espn-body-issue-2013-posing-athletes-whose-popularity-will-skyrocket.

Cromwell, Howard Casey and Jaak Panksepp (2011) 'Rethinking the cognitive revolution from a neural perspective: How overuse/misuse of the term "cognition" and the neglect of affective controls in behavior neuroscience could be delaying progress in understanding the BrainMind', *Neuroscience and Biobehavioral Reviews*, 35(2011), pp. 2026–2035. Available online at: http://www.crossfit.com/cf-info/what-crossfit.html, http://www.forbes.com/sites/davidtao/2013/06/02/how-crossfit-embraced-fans-and-became-the-next-great-spectator-sport/.

Glassman, Available online at: https://www.youtube.com/watch?v=-EBOXy BUI0U. Also see 'Do Not Cross CrossFit', Inc.com, http://www.inc.com/magazine/201307/burt-helm/crossfit-empire.html.

Grosz, Elizabeth (2010) 'Feminism, materialism, and freedom', in Diana Coole and Samantha Frost (eds) *New Materialisms: Ontology, Agency, Politics.* Durham: Duke UP, pp. 139–157.

Heywood, Leslie (1998) *Bodymakers: A Cultural Anatomy of Women's Bodybuilding.* New Brunswick: Rutgers UP.

Heywood, Leslie (2007) 'Producing girls: Empire, sport, and the neoliberal body', in Jennifer Hargreaves and Patricia Vertinsky (eds) *Physical Culture, Power, and the Body.* New York: Routledge, pp. 101–120.

Heywood, Leslie and Shari Dworkin (2000) *Built to Win: The Female Athlete as Cultural Icon.* Minnesota: University of Minnesota Press.

Leys, Ruth (2011) 'The turn to affect: A critique', *Critical Inquiry*, 37(3), pp. 434–472.

Moore, Kelly (2013) 'Fear and fun: Science and gender, emotion and embodiment under neoliberalism', in Elizabeth Bernstein and Janet R. Jakobsen (eds) *The Scholar and the Feminist Online* (11.1–11.2 Fall 2012/Spring 2013).

Panksepp, Jaak (1998) *Affective Neuroscience.* Oxford and New York: Oxford UP.

Panksepp, Jaak (2000) 'Emotions as natural kinds within the mammalian brain', in M. Lewis and J. M. Haviland-Jones (eds) *Handbook of Emotions.* 2nd Edition, New York: The Guilford Press, pp. 137–156.

Panksepp, Jaak and Lucy Biven (2012) *The Archaeology of Mind: The Neuroevolutionary Origins of Human Emotions.* New York: Norton.

Papoulias, Constantina and Felicity Callard (2010) 'Biology's gift: Interrogating the turn to affect', *Body & Society*, 16(29).

Porges, Stephen (2011) *The Polyvagal Theory: Neurophysiological Foundations of Emotions, Attachment, Communication, and Self-Regulation.* New York: Norton. Available online at: http://r23nikita.blogspot.com/2012/10/strong-is-new-bautiful.html.

Rose, Nicholas (2013) 'The human sciences in a biological age', *Theory, Culture & Society*, 30(1), 3–34, p. 4. Available online at: http://sfonline.barnard.edu/gender-justice-and-neoliberal-transformations/fear-and-fun-science-and-gender-emotion-and-embodiment-under-neoliberalism/.

Thrift, Nicholas (2004) 'Intensities of feeling: Towards a spatial politics of affect', *Geografiska Annaler*, 86B(1), 57–78. Available online at: https://www.youtube.com/watch?v=5zvqNHDTf8Y, https://www.youtube.com/watch?v=4_ymRxOqo8U.

3
Big Sister TV: Bossiness, Bullying and Banter in Early Twenty-first Century Make-over Television

Angela Smith

Make-over television shows became one of the defining genres of early twenty-first century television across the Western world. From their small beginnings in 15-minute slots on daytime TV in the late 1990s, by the end of the first decade of the twenty-first century they had come to dominate primetime TV and even have their own devoted network and cable channels. A common feature of all of these shows has been the prevalence of female subjects to be 'made over'. As Rosalind Gill (2007) has observed, the body is promoted as integral to female identity, and thus is a site for postfeminist attention where a woman's pursuit of beauty engages both her consumer power and her self-governance. If, as Angela McRobbie (2009) attests, postfeminism is linked with vocabulary of 'freedom', 'choice' and 'empowerment', then these shows are underpinned by the assumption that the participants have made the 'wrong' choice, and thus are in need of stern guidance if they are ever to achieve the 'empowerment' that postfeminism promotes through the female body. What characterized these make-overs is the use of bullying, bossy tactics by the hosts and tears by the subject as they progress on their 'journey' to a better, more stylish self. This chapter will suggest that, while the bullying of the earlier shows has diminished, there nevertheless remains an underpinning strategy of humiliation that is accompanied by a more dissipated sense of belligerency throughout such shows as the female body continues to be open to surveillance.

Make-over shows have recently become the subject of much academic attention, with a special issue of the *Journal of Media and Cultural Studies* edited by Tania Lewis in 2008 being devoted to a discussion of them. The fact that such shows have an overwhelmingly feminine agenda can be related to the way in which the panoptic gaze of contemporary culture is very distinctively gendered. Elizabeth Spelman (1982) has pointed out that, historically, where men have been judged in terms of what their bodies can do, women are thought of primarily in terms of how their bodies look. In Sandra Bartky's much-quoted passage, she identifies some of the facets of this gaze:

> The woman who checks her make-up half a dozen times a day to see if her foundation of has caked or her mascara run, who worried that the wind or rain may spoil her hairdo, who looks frequently to see if her stockings have bagged at the ankle, or who, feeling fat, monitors everything she eats, has become, just as surely as the inmate of the panopticon, a self-policing subject, a self committed to a relentless, self-surveillance. This self-surveillance is a form of obedience to patriarchy.
>
> (Bartky, 1990, p. 80)

The televisual manifestation of such surveillance is in shows which feature 'ordinary persons, people ostensibly plucked from the population and held up as exemplars of the ordinary and embodiments of an issue' (Bonner, 2003: 86–89) as their most important component. These members of the public are made over by hosts/experts who are specialists in some aspect of everyday life (such as fashion or personal grooming), whose 'principle role is to guide the ordinary persons through a series of consumer choices in order to achieve a particular goal' (Redden, 2007, p. 152), typically an 'improvement' in their personal appearance. The underlying assumption is that the current self is always in need of improvement, and that the expert host is the person to guide the participants to this goal. Ann Kibbey, for example, has suggested that the authority of the expert in such shows relies on the assumption that they are instrumental in changing ordinary people into something that is different, where the old self by default is viewed as being inadequate (2005, p. 15). As the papers published in the special issue of the *Journal of Media and Cultural Studies* show, a common thread in these make-over shows is that of governmentality, a thread that underpins such shows around the globe. This usually manifests itself in what Guy Redden (2008) refers to as the 'reflexive individualisation' of citizens via the formation of self-governing consumer-citizens 'through teaching audiences to adopt and value particular modes of reflexivity in their daily lives' (Lewis, 2002, p. 444). The participants are encouraged to make the 'right choices' which, as Redden says, are 'represented as ones through which the participant may both claim personal satisfaction and demonstrate their enhanced worth to others' (Redden, 2008, p. 488).

Bullying head girls as presenters

The fact that, internationally, it is usually women who are the subject of such make-overs leads us to view these shows through a postfeminism lens. As discussed elsewhere (Weber and Tice, 2009; Smith, 2010, 2013), there is a middle-class, white bias in the favoured 'taste' of the make-over, and this can be related to the strand of postfeminism that seeks to regain the traditional forms of gendered behaviour that the second wave feminist movement dismissed. Referred to as 'new traditionalism' or 'lady power' (Smith, 2013), this discourse of empowerment through personal styling is one that underpins the aim of the make-over: to rekindle a love life, to get a better job, to gain confidence after some life tragedy. Thus the successful make-over features a woman who assumes the appearance of middle-class feminine consumerism, in 'Cinderella-cum-makeover narratives' (Kathryn Fraser, 2007, p. 18) in which there is a promise of transformation from a problematized subject to one that is open to social mobility through the powers of consumption. While the various studies of make-over shows all point to this conclusion, either explicitly or implicitly, they do not tend to focus on the means by which such advice is given. The purpose of this paper, therefore, is to add to this discussion of make-over shows by looking in some detail at the strategies used by the experts on such shows in order to suggest that a shift in presentational style can be linked to wider social changes in the first decade of the twenty-first century.

Lisa Taylor, in her discussion of lifestyle make-over television programmes, has pointed to the place they have taken in the schedules where previously sitcoms and dramas would have been shown. She argues that they have adopted some of the main features of such shows, in particular 'drama, conflict, emotion and stereotypes' (2002, p. 489). This paper seeks to examine recent developments in the 'conflict and emotion' found in such programmes. As Angela McRobbie (2009), Gareth Palmer (2004) and others have suggested elsewhere, such TV is usually characterized by bullying strategies employed by the expert host. For example, in the early part of this century, this is associated in the UK with the mediated performances of hosts such as Gillian McKeith of *You Are What You Eat* and the *10 Years Younger* presenter Nicki Hambleton-Jones (both Channel 4) as well as the various style-related programmes hosted by stylists Trinny Woodhall and Susannah Constantine. McRobbie in particular has been interested in how make-over shows legitimize forms of class antagonism, particularly between women where 'aggressive words and disparaging gestures' are features of competitiveness. She asks how women actually compete with each other in such programmes, and concludes:

> The answer provided by these programmes relies on a return to old-fashioned 'school-girl' styles of feminine bitchiness, rivalry and contemporary popular entertainment. But what this means is that public enactments of hatred and animosity are refracted at a bodily or corporeal level against weaker and much less powerful people, with impunity, on the grounds that the insult is made in a playful spirit and that it is not really meant.
>
> (2009, p. 130)

As McRobbie suggests, we are thus meant to read the bullying as being ironic or insincere, at least intended for the benefit of the participants while ultimately being for the entertainment of the viewers. However, the overall perception on viewing such programmes is one of bullying and bossiness. This links with work by Penelope Brown and Stephen Levinson who draw on the work of Erving Goffman with regard to our social, public persona, referred to as 'face'. In this way, the abstract notion of 'face' is linked to 'two specific kinds of desire ("face wants") attributed by interactants to one another: the desire to be unimpeded in one's actions (negative face), and the desire (in some respects) to be approved of (positive face)' (Brown and Levinson, 1987, p. 13). In this model of politeness theory, as explained by Brown and Levinson (1978, 1987), we can understand friendship and solidarity as something that is characterized linguistically by humour, compliments and personal comments, referred to by Brown and Levinson as 'positive politeness'. The concept of 'negative politeness' does not carry the lay value judgement of 'rudeness', but instead can be seen to orientate away from solidarity towards greater social distance. Any utterance which runs contrary to the face wants of the addressee and/or the speaker and thus threatens the face is termed a 'face threatening act', or FTA (see Brown and Levinson, 1987, p. 65). Where face comes into the equation for our purposes here is in relation to the interpretation of these linguistic strategies by the interactants. For example, in the following extract (Table 3.1) from *What Not to Wear* (BBC1, 5 December 2006), presented by Trinny Woodhall and Susannah Constantine, the hapless participant's attempt at self-mockery (attending to her own positive face wants) is greeted with stern reproach:

Extract 1

Table 3.1 What Not to Wear: Trinny, Susannah and Hayley watch video playback

Participant (Hayley – H) sitting on sofa with Trinny (T) and Susannah (S) either side of her, watching secretly filmed footage of her in various unfashionable outfits (vo = voice-over).

T	You look like you've just crawled out of bed	Shot of Hayley wearing multi-coloured coat, shopping	1
H	I do look a state don't I really	Shots of Hayley on sofa in studio with Trinny and	5
T	Mmm	Susannah	
H	[laughs nervously] It's my Joseph coat of amazing colours		
			10
S	Why are you laughing? [not laughing]		
H	Because everyone else does [quietly, slightly laughing]		15
T (vo)	Time for the 360 degree mirror (.) where Hayley can see herself (.) from *every* angle	Shots of Hayley entering mirrored chamber	

Trinny's FTA on lines 1–2 is taken as a positive politeness strategy by Hayley, who agrees with her, then goes on to make a joke at her own expense by comparing the colourful jumper with a well-known theatrical garment from the re-telling of the biblical tale (lines 8–9). Her nervous laughter at this point seems like an attempt on her part to engage with Trinny and Susannah on their own terms of criticism of her, drawing on positive politeness strategies to minimize the social distance between them. However, Susannah's unlaughing reproach on line 11 rejects Hayley's attempt at humour and thus reframes the positive politeness strategy as an FTA. Hayley's somewhat plaintive confession on line 14 does not elicit a compassionate response but instead the voice-over moves the scene on to the mirrored chamber. This mirrored chamber allows for the participant to see themselves from all angles, and the camera is positioned so as to allow viewers to act as voyeurs as the participant nervously looks at themselves from this unconventional angle. Trinny and Susannah wait outside the chamber for the first few seconds, but then open the door behind the participant and commence their commentary on her appearance (Table 3.2).

Extract 2

Table 3.2   Hayley enters the mirror chamber

H	It's not as bad as I thought it was going to be	Hayley enters mirrored chamber wearing brightly coloured jumper.	1
S	You are seriously disturbed		
			5
T	Are you on drugs?	T&S enter mirror chamber, gaze at Hayley's clothes but don't	
H	[laughing nervously]	make eye contact with her	
T	Not as bad as you thought it was going to be (.) [shouting] are you mad are you totally out of your mind?		10
H	It's still not bad (.) it's kind of bright it's the sort of thing you could wear (2), er, in the summer		15

S	Do you know what (.) if I'm going to be completely frank which I will be (.) you look like a hunchback in that		20
H	[laughs nervously, fidgeting under their gaze]		25
S	You look like you've got no neck you look like your head is growing straight from your shoulders because of that collar (.) it's completely the wrong shape (.) if it was tighter (.) yes (.) if it was right down there [pulls at neckline] yes (.) that does no (.5) service to you whatsoever no one there's not one single good thing about that top not one	Spulls at jumper to make more figure-hugging	30 35
T	Come on (.) out you get (.) next outfit	Hayley plods despondently out.	40

Hayley's attempt to defend her wardrobe choice (having previously identified the colourful jumper as one of her favourite items of clothing) through hedging on line 1 is immediately countered by the voices of the presenters outside of the chamber. Assuming positions of mock indignation, they draw hypothetical doubts as to the sanity of the participant in their habitual performance of exasperation. Again, Hayley attempts to treat this as a positive politeness strategy by laughing, but Trinny's performance of escalating annoyance is demonstrated in her raised voice (lines 11–12) that again calls into question Hayley's mental state. Hayley's attempted defence of her outfit draws on the social world in which she lives as she suggests occasions on which she could wear it (lines 15–17), but again employs hedging in repeating her belief that the outfit is 'not bad'. This is rejected by Susannah, who draws on an unfavourable physical metaphor (lines 20–21) that is framed as candid advice, the sort of positive politeness strategy a close friend might employ. Hayley's continued discomfort is clear as she physically fidgets and squirms under the gaze and verbal assault of Trinny and Susannah. As Susannah reaches into the chamber and starts to pull at the clothing, she offers a commentary that demolishes Hayley's defence of her clothing without allowing any further intervention from the wearer. Trinny judges the top duly condemned and issues a directive to Hayley to step out of the chamber and put on her next outfit for the whole process to be repeated (line 39–40).

The overall strategy of bullying is aligned with the determination to 'improve' the appearance of the participant, as shown later in this episode where Hayley disagrees with the choice of outfit Trinny and Susannah have selected for her (Table 3.3).

Extract 3

Table 3.3   Trinny and Susannah criticize Hayley's choice of outfit

S	Oh (.) divine	Hayley emerges from cubicle pulling uncomfortably at skirt	1
T	Look at you (.) you've lost a stone		
S	You really have	T&S stand with hands on hips leaning against wall.	5
H	But the skirt the skirt looks like my mum's (.) it's the vile material that my mother wore and I don't I don't (.) like the skirt		10
S	[incredulously] Wh- wh- what childhood nightmare did you go through to make you think that's a vile fabric		15
H	[laughs nervously but frustratedly] I don't I don't like the skirt (.) I like the top but I don't like the skirt	Hayley stands uncomfortably with hands behind back	20
T	I really am beyond understanding you (.) this is the best shaped skirt you have put on (.) today (1) by far because your tummy's flat it skims your hips you look thinner	Hayley kicks feet uncomfortably	25
H	It doesn't do anything for me at all		30
T	It does so much for you I can't tell you		

H	I know but it doesn't for me it doesn't for me		35
T	I know but this is your perfect shaped skirt (.) perfect length and shape (1)	Hayley retreats to changing cubicle	40
S	But if we're not going to persuade you we are not going to persuade you (.) it's your loss	T&S look exhaustedly at one another	45
T	Exactly (.) ok (2) Oh God [sitting on floor]		
S	It depresses me actually (.) it's so it's really I find it really frustrating		50
T	Yeh		
S	That she can't see it		55

Hayley's physical discomfort is clear from her defiant posture (standing with hands behind her back, kicking her feet around), while the sense of physical confrontation is emphasized by Trinny and Susannah's stance of leaning back against the changing room walls with hands on hips. Hayley's rejection of the compliments paid by Trinny and Susannah (lines 1 and 3) is supported by her vehement dislike of the skirt she has been made to wear. She repeats her objection ('I don't like the skirt' is repeated on lines 10, 17 and 18) with an increasing sense of exasperation and discomfort, again employing the positive politeness strategy of laughter as a defence mechanism but with the same ineffectual result. Trinny again implies there is something mentally deficient with the participant (line 21), this FTA rather at odds with the compliments that it follows. While Hayley attempts to acknowledge the superior wisdom of the stylists (lines 31–32), she maintains her dislike of the garment by repeating her assertion that she simply does not like it. The confrontation ends with Hayley's silent discomfort and Susannah's double-voiced recognition of defeat (lines 39–41) that is to Hayley's detriment not theirs. As Hayley retreats to the changing cubicle, the camera shows Trinny slumped to the floor as Susannah frames this not as a defeat but as a rejection of their good advice as stylists by one who needs to learn but won't.

Such bullying and bossiness is characteristic of Trinny and Susannah's approach to styling members of the public, with no overt element of fun being allowed to creep into their stern, head girl performances. Physically, they are often some distance from the participant, such as in Extract 1 (Table 3.1) where they are seated on an L-shaped sofa but not within reach of one another. Elsewhere, physical contact comes only in the pulling and tugging of clothing. The personal well-being of the participant does not appear to be their concern at this point, and if anything they are responsible for unmitigated FTAs which call attention to the emotional fragility of their candidates.

The widespread prevalence of such belligerent strategies across make-over programmes from the early part of the twenty-first century could be said to reflect the confidence and consumerist flamboyance of this period (see Higgins et al., 2012). However, this confidence and ostentation have been dramatically disrupted since late 2007 with the onset of the so-called 'credit crunch'. This coincides with a downturn in the fortunes of Trinny and Susannah (viewing figures for their UK show *What Not to Wear* dropped from 6.7 million in 2007 to just over 2 million when they transferred the format to ITV1 in 2008), as the media seemed to tire of their bossiness. Writing in *The Independent* in 2008, Carla Long observed:

> When Trinny and Susannah first hit our screens with What Not To Wear in the early Noughties, their dominatrix-style bossiness and tendency to grapple with women's breasts as part of their programme of public humiliation seemed daringly abrasive.
>
> (*The Independent*, 20 August 2008)

This implicit fatigue (triggered by 'seemed') with their style of presenting coincided with the arrival on UK screens of a new stylist, the overtly gay and resolutely populist Gok Wan. Gok Wan's show *How to Look Good Naked* (2006–2010) was first broadcast on Channel 4 in June 2006, the second series a year later and then subsequently at six-monthly intervals. The format has been taken up in other countries, where gay-identifying male stylists often act as presenters (*Queer Eye for the Straight Guy* presenter Carson Kressley hosts the US version on Lifetime Television). Wan's various make-over and style-related shows on Channel 4 continue the format commonly found in other shows, but he is held up in the media as being every woman's gay best friend, a refreshingly friendly change from the bullying and hectoring of Trinny and Susannah.

The print media lauded Wan's style of presentation, while also recognizing that the format of the make-over shows Trinny and Susannah had pioneered was superficially unchanged. In common with the vast majority of make-over shows, the format comprises:

- Introduction of the participant, problematizing their appearance.
- Ritual stripping out of unfavourable clothing and other elements of appearance.
- Intervention of professional stylists.
- 'The reveal' (Moseley, 2000), where the participant sees their made-over self for the first time.
- The 'validation' (Smith, 2010), where the finished product is evaluated by relevant contributors.

The host/stylist's intervention can be said to be the focal point for belligerency, particularly where the hosts strip down the problematized participant in a humiliating way that is meant to be read as part of the fixing process. This is particularly the case in the 'mirrored chamber' scene that is a characteristic of Trinny and Susannah's shows. The linguistic strategies adopted at this point by Trinny and Susannah and other stylists is what has attracted much criticism, and seems to be regarded as the main difference between them and Gok Wan. For example, an article in *The Guardian* seeks to be disparaging towards the style of Trinny and Susannah, while humanizing Gok Wan:

> [Trinny and Susannah] may occasionally talk about their past problems but are too full of braying self-confidence to convince Mavis from Surbiton that they were once like her. Instead, they come across as a gorgon-headed beast of matronly, imperious bossiness. Wan, however, was once an obese bullied teenager who made himself over to resemble a Chinese Jarvis Cocker and somehow convinced the world that he is a fashion expert and every woman's gay best friend.
>
> (*The Guardian*, 20 August 2008)

Although the typical bullying of ordinary members of the public has been considerably moderated by Wan, other belligerent strategies remain. Rachel Cooke claimed in *The Observer* (November 2007), 'Gok isn't into humiliation, and his programme does not include any element of it.' However, I would suggest that humiliation of members of the public is actually very much part of his shows, and other strategies we could categorize as being belligerent appear elsewhere in the programme.

Notably, the format of Wan's shows have a nod towards celebrity culture and routinely feature 'celebrity guests' from the field of popular and light entertainment television. In particular, we will focus on the magazine show *Gok's Fashion Fix* (analysing one episode that was first broadcast on 19 May 2009), which is hosted by the eponymous Gok and centres around a weekly make-over. What we will suggest is that the overtly belligerent strategies in these shows are now directed not at members of the public, but at other guests on the show, guests who are less susceptible to the public humiliation that characterized the strategies used by earlier hosts.

Humiliation? Every woman's gay best friend

To begin with Gok Wan's gendered performance, he uses his openly gay status to legitimize his role as stylist, drawing on the stereotypes of gay style. Wan's arrival on TV coincides with the appearance of gay men as hosts/experts in other shows internationally, such as *Queer Eye for the Straight Guy* in the US. As Richardson and Waring (2013, p. 97) point out, 'the way gay male culture polices body image and the way patriarchal culture controls female body image' makes it unsurprising that the 'most popular make-over shows in recent years have been those in which the stylist/make-over expert is a gay man'. By the turn of the century, the visibility of gay storylines in fictional TV drama had moved on from the coming-out narratives found in soaps of the 1990s to being centre stage. For example, in the UK, the much-discussed drama *Queer as Folk* (Channel 4, 1999–2000) centred around the lives of young gay men in Manchester (see Munt, 2000; Thornham and Purvis, 2005; Davis, 2009), while the hugely popular New York-based sitcom *Will and Grace* (NBC 1998–2006) featured the straight-acting homosexual Will and his flamboyant gay friend Jack. Their relationship with the heterosexual Grace and her friend Karen show what Shugart has suggested is a 'gay male privilege' attached to the representation of gay men that we can also see in Gok Wan's performance.

> Due to their homosexuality, they (gay men) can touch women with impunity in inappropriate ways and inappropriate contexts – this may entail overt, very intimate sexual touches, public contexts, or access to women who would conventionally be construed as sexually unavailable. This consistent pattern cultivates a perception of gay male sexuality as an extension of homosexual privilege; the access and license portrayed in these representations is tantamount to a degree of sexual entitlement that is, notably, no longer readily available to heterosexual men.
>
> (Shugart, 2003, p. 83)

This homosexual performance thus allows a biologically male stylist to avoid the accusations of sexual impropriety that straight male stylists might be open to if they engaged with personal intimacy with members of the public. Wan's close physical contact, which is articulated as 'grabbing women's breasts' by critics of Trinny and Susannah, is rendered acceptable and not 'bitchy' or bullying as it is seen as more playful through his performance. As Linda McLoughlin (2013) points out, somewhat disconcertingly, he often refers to himself in the third person, drawing attention to his sexuality. For example, he punningly refers to himself as the Fairy Gok-mother, Aunty Gok, and 'your queen in shining glamour'. This enhances his knowingly ironic gay performance. His participants are gorgeous, fantastic, adorable, luscious – adjectives Robin Lakoff (2004) would suggest are typically feminine. These are used positively to enhance the self-confidence of participants. If linguistically Wan presents himself as being feminine and friendly, as McLoughlin has suggested, there are still links to the humiliation of earlier shows. For example, in *What Not To Wear*, the mirror chamber scene, as we saw above, requires the participant to strip to her underwear and be viewed from all angles while being subjected to a highly uncomfortable commentary by the hosts. However, as McLoughlin points out, 'in Wan's use of this device, the tearful participants are consoled with hugs and expressions of concern by the presenter' (2013, p. 14). What I would suggest, though, is that this ritual humiliation remains central to such shows and continues to provide a discursive space for the participant to experience a great deal of discomfort, as evidenced by their heightened emotionality at this point.

In the show we are going to at look in more detail, *Gok's Fashion Fix*, the magazine format centres around the weekly make-over of a member of the public, who is always female, straight and nearly always middle-aged. The other elements of the show will be discussed shortly, but first we will look at how Wan interacts with his 'ordinary' participant as part of the instructional fable which Redden (2007) and others identify as being central to such make-over shows.

In the interaction between Wan and participants, we find directives use humour that is encapsulated in Wan's own camp on-screen persona of the stylist/best friend. Bald, on-record directives are therefore out of character for Wan, so the effect is ameliorated. For example, in his opening direct-to-camera scene, Wan employs directives towards the general viewers:

> GW: OK girls I've got a brand new mantra (.) shop less but wear more (.) it's time to put a stop to all that wasteful shopping and cluttered closets (3) and this week I'm in Exmouth in Devon to meet my biggest clutter culprit yet (2) forty-six year old Anne-Marie James is stuck in a fashion rut (3)

The directives appear in his direct-to-camera address to viewers before focusing on the participant, thus framing the show as being specifically about one make-over but nevertheless applicable to a widespread problem that is built into Wan's common-sense assumption that such a dilemma exists. Here, Wan is addressing specifically female viewers ('girls' is used as a discourse marker to identify specific absent audience members), and the lack of hedging or other mitigating strategies in 'it's time to put a stop to all that wasteful shopping and cluttered closets' carries the assumption that such a context is universal among his identified audience. This message of curtailing extravagant expenditure while promoting prudent consumer spending links with the wider social concerns relating to the recession that was just beginning to take effect at this time. As viewers, we meet Anne-Marie through a series of vox pops that show her confessing to her 'crime' of not discarding out-of-fashion clothes. Immediately before we see Wan and Anne-Marie meet face to face on screen for the first time, Wan's voice-over invites viewers to join in his ironic disgust at her wardrobe as we see shots of her clothes hung on a washing line that the production team have strung across a public park.

> GW: Cue your queen in shining glamour (1) this serial hoarder is about to be purged of the past (2) so this is our biggest clothes line to date (.) Anne-Marie has got so many clothes I have got over two hundred foot of washing line (.) now get a load of Anne-Marie's wardrobe past and present

The directive here – 'get a load of Anne-Marie's wardrobe' – employs colloquial language to enhance a shared sense of incredulity that follows the somewhat vague statistic about the length of a washing line. This colloquial language, which is accompanied by journalistic punning and alliteration, is typical of Wan's scripted direct-to-camera talk and has an implicit link to popular fashion magazines such as *Glamour* and *Grazia*, which this programme has more explicit links with elsewhere (e.g., in the vox pops from the various fashion editors of these magazines who comment on current style trends).

This leads us to look in more detail at the format of the show and the way in which it includes the ritual humiliation of the public participant. In Wan's case, a very public forum is being used. In the extract shown in Table 3.4, Anne-Marie, is seen arriving in a public park where Wan's team have hung her clothes out, apparently without her knowing (Table 3.4).

Extract 4

Table 3.4   Gok's Fashion Fix: Anne-Marie enters park

AM	Oh my God (3) Oh my God (2) [hands to mouth, laughing nervously] I think I recognize some of that	Close-up of AM's face intercut with shots of clothes on washing line	1
			5
GW	Hi! [greets AM and puts arm around her shoulders]		

Figure 3.1 Gok Wan greets Anne-Marie

The participant, after initial shock, adopts the role of supplicant to this humiliation and plays along (line 2). Wan's appearance in the scene is a performance of friendship and close physical contact as part of his performance of friendship that is far from the bullying and hectoring of earlier hosts. Still with his arm supportive around Anne-Marie's shoulders, he stands beside her surveying the washing line of clothes and sets out the strategy for this part of the make-over (see Figure 3.1 and Table 3.5).

Extract 5

Table 3.5 Gok's Fashion Fix: Gok and Anne-Marie sort out clothing

GW	We're going to be ruthless (.) if it doesn't fit you	Close shot of AM and GW standing together looking at washing line. GW's arm around AM's shoulders.	1
AM	Yeh		
			5
GW	It's going		
AM	Yeh		

What is noticeable is that Wan uses the collective pronoun to include himself in the symbolic stripping of the clothes from the washing line (line 1). This ameliorates the force of the directive, and also aligns himself with the participant rather than distancing himself as Trinny and Susannah were seen to do. A similar amelioration occurs in the extract shown in Table 3.6, when Wan is seen interrupting Anne-Marie, repeating her own words ('never wear those') to impose the symbolic violence of removing the clothes (Table 3.6):

Extract 6

Table 3.6   Gok's Fashion Fix: Gok and Anne-Marie sort out clothing

AM	I never wear those because I think	AM points to clothes on line which GW pulls off theatrically and throws to the ground.	1
GW	You never wear those (.) pull them off pull them off (.) come on girl		5
AM	They fit me on the waist and the bum	AM pulls at a pair of trousers.	10
GW	So these don't then	GW pulls at another pair of trousers	
AM	No but these do but		
GW	So these don't		15
AM	They do [laughing]		
GW	So these don't then (.) no no don't you dare lie to me (2) oh God this feels good (1) I'm free I'm free	Pulling trousers off the line and dancing around clothes on the ground.	20

His directives on lines 5–6 are ameliorated by the joint act of pulling the clothes off the washing line, acting as an invitation to join in with him. Anne-Marie's attempt to retain some of her clothing on the grounds that it fits her is rejected by Wan, whose rejection-insistence argument strategy echoes that found in Amy Sheldon's (1990) work on young boys arguing, and here reflects Wan's childishly camp persona as he dances around the pile of clothes in a comic nod to ritual cleansing (lines 20–21). This also serves to ameliorate his directive on line 20 where he adopts a stern persona to reprimand Anne-Marie for a hypothetical lie. It is important here to notice also that Anne-Marie is seen to be playing along with this, marked by her positive politeness strategy of laughter on line 17.

Wan's behaviour, which results in the humiliation of the public participant, underpins his authority as stylist, as is found with Trinny and Susannah. At the end of this scene, Wan and Anne-Marie are again shown standing side by side, with Wan's arm around her shoulders as they survey the large pile of discarded clothes seen on the muddy grass in the park (Table 3.7).

Extract 7

Table 3.7 Gok's Fashion Fix: Gok and Anne-Marie survey discarded clothing

GW	How are you feeling?	GW standing with arm around AM's shoulders, intercut with shots of discarded clothing lying on the ground.	1
AM	Sick (.) really really sick (1) It's just such a big thing to do (.) it I would never have done this without a real shove (1) and it's done.		5

Physically, Wan further ameliorates the humiliation by his physical performance of intimate friendship with hugs and close contact that follows the more humiliating physical performance of throwing clothes to the ground. The scene ends with Anne-Marie reaffirming the legitimacy of this strategy and also her espousal of it. Wan emerges from the scene with his gay best friend status accentuated, his use of directives seemingly employed cooperatively and with humour. Attention to what Heidegger refers to as a 'structure of care' (1962) is very clearly shown to be important in Wan's performance. Thus there are differences between Wan and earlier hosts such as Trinny and Susannah, but ultimately the same public humiliation has been ritualized, here in a far more public form through the display of the participant's clothes in a park.

Banter and bullying

Elsewhere in the show, belligerence is performed in a more overtly argumentative way. For example, in *Gok's Fashion Fix* there is a running thread of competitiveness with American stylist Brix Smart-Smith, where banter is used to enhance their friendship-between-equals status. Each week, Wan and Smart-Smith are challenged to contrive outfits for a catwalk show based around a certain context, for example summer beach holiday, a night out. Wan, champion of the lower middle classes, shops in the High Street, while Smart-Smith has a seemingly unlimited budget to buy designer wear. The spectators of the catwalk show vote for their favourite set of clothes (Wan nearly always wins). In Table 3.8, which shows an extract from the opening of the episode, Wan and Smart-Smith are shown walking down a shopping street in bantering conversation, discussing the competitiveness between them. The reference to the dog relates to a pug dog that is usually seen as a fashion accessory to Smart-Smith, but here unaccountably is being carried by Wan (see Figure 3.2 and Table 3.8).

Figure 3.2   Gok Wan and Brix Smart-Smith engaging in banter

Extract 8

Table 3.8   Gok's Fashion Fix: Gok and Brix Smart-Smith

GW	Brix (1) I won last week and I've got your sodding dog	Walking down shopping street, GW carrying 'high street' logo carrier bags and BSS's pug dog,	1
BSS	You are winning (.) by a hair's breadth (.) by just a few votes (.) I'm so close to beating you	BSS carrying 'designer label' carrier bags.	5
GW	The public like the High Street they're the ones that's voting (.) just give up		10

Mildly taboo language ('your sodding dog', line 2) reinforces the FTAs in their banter. Wan aligns himself with the general public who can't afford designer clothes, here explicitly through the reference to the public vote on the catwalk show (lines 8–9), and Wan's colloquial, mildly taboo language serves to further align him as 'one of us' rather than belonging to the exclusive world of fashion. However, McRobbie's observation about make-over shows being a legitimized form of class antagonism is rendered implicitly true here as the competition between Wan and Smart-Smith centres around Wan's ability to reproduce 'designer' wear cheaply from high street stores

Weekly celebrity guests allow for further engagement with banter; however, there is the complication of Wan here performing as professional stylist to uninformed guest. Often, this takes the form of Wan acting as big sister/childminder to the guest who takes on the role of the naughty child, in a similar way to stylists Trinny and Susannah in their interaction with 'ordinary participants', which in their case was framed as bossy and bitchy. The celebrity guests on Wan's shows are nearly always people who have well-defined synthetic personalities on reality TV, such as Ruby Wax, Davina McCall and Lorraine Kelly. In using reality TV stars rather than actors, there is another nod towards less exclusivity, but with a strategic twist, as we will see. It also means that these are personalities who inhabit an on-screen persona that transfers across contexts rather than is anchored into a specific text, as with an actor. This allows them to continue their on-screen performances in a different, everyday context, with the added element of their being taken out of their usual environment and thus having the excuse to behave in an unconventional yet believable way. The resultant childish, unruly performance when shopping implies that the celebrity does not know the rules of normal high street behaviour as they are above such mundanity. To examine one such guest in a little more detail, we will look at Wan's interaction with comedian Ruby Wax (Table 3.9).

Extract 9

Table 3.9 Gok's Fashion Fix: Gok and Ruby Wax

GW	[indirect aside] She's going to get me into so much trouble [to RW] Ruby (.) you can't steal the display	RW clambers onto display and attempts to remove non-clothing items	1
			5
RW	What about the wig (1) the wig would be good (1) and the rope isn't bad	RW removes wig from mannequin	
GW	No Ruby no (.) Ruby Ruby (.) Ruby now		10
RW	You said I could have what I wanted [petulant]	RW wanders away carrying wig	
			15
GW	Come on (.) you can't have the display [indirect aside] I need to get her to focus on clothes before we get thrown out	GW sits on side of display with head in hands	

Wan's indirect aside strategy (line 1–2) serves to maintain a level of authenticity and spontaneity that differs from his scripted direct-to-camera talk where he is able to perform the polished professional presenter/stylist who is in total command of the show (see Higgins et al., 2012). In this case, it is Wan's feigned inability to control a guest celebrity who is behaving in an uncooperative manner, leaving him alone on camera as his guest refuses to play by the make-over game rules of the authoritative, all-knowing stylist host. This lack of cooperation is shown visually as Wax runs around the shop grabbing armfuls of clothes apparently without regard for style or size. Such childish impatience is not expected of adults in a shopping environment, and this is emphasized by Wan's indirect aside speech that emphasizes the lack of socialization, which is unacceptable.

When talking to Wax, he employs direct speech acts and unmitigated directives ('you can't steal the display' lines 3–4; 'you can't have the display' lines 16–17) and the repetition of the bald, on-record FTA 'No Ruby, no, Ruby Ruby...' (line 10) which positions him as an adult reacting to an unruly child (see Figure 3.3). As McTear and others have shown, such as strategy is typical of child-directed speech employed by caregivers to very young children. Here, the strategy as employed by Wan seems provoked by the immature performance of Wax. Wan, in the more powerful role of stylist/big sister, assumes responsibility for Wax's actions, as seen on lines 17–19, where such a failure on his part is theatrically predicted to result in their joint expulsion from the store. This authority over Wax is also found in line 2, where he implies this responsibility for her, and is also found in Wax's utterance on lines 13–14.

Here, Wan is not the 'gay best friend' to the participant, but a somewhat thwarted professional who is forced to adopt a more authoritative persona employing a more bullying strategy in order to maintain his position as expert stylist. However, there is still an emphasis on female celebrity participants who are in need of styling advice and, where they seek to reject such advice, as with Wax's performance here, the resultant banter between equals is again edited to highlight conflict as entertainment.

Figure 3.3   Gok Wan and Ruby Wax

Conclusions

While women continue to be bombarded with messages implying their inadequacy and therefore the need to reinvent themselves, make-over shows such as those discussed here dominate the media, all following the same basic structure. The dramatic potential of such shows ensures that they attract viewers and never seem short of members of the public who wish to be 'made over'. However, the way in which such transformational narratives are presented to viewers is changing in some cases. The bullying and hectoring of hosts such as Trinny and Susannah towards members of the public has largely been moderated in the performance of stylists like Gok Wan, who evokes the 'gay male privilege' that allows him to hold and touch women in a way that would not be appropriate for a male hetero-sexual presenter. That said, other strategies of belligerency, such as banter and bullying, do still exist for entertainment purposes in the less contentious sections of the show where he engages with fellow media professionals. More troubling, though, is the continuation of the ritual humiliation of the public participant. While Trinny and Susannah infamously used to strip their participants in a mirrored chamber, Wan performs humiliation in a more public forum, in this episode's case, by hanging out the participant's clothes in the local park. (On his other shows, as McLoughlin has described, such as *How to Look Good Naked*, the humiliation of the participant again uses a public forum such as parading large photographs of the partially clothed participant around the streets, and culminating in a lingerie fashion show where every participant is compelled by the show's convention to strip to her underwear in a packed shopping centre.) Elsewhere, Nicki Hambleton-Jones has been replaced as presenter of the UK version of *10 Years Younger* by Myleene Klass, who first appeared as a co-presenter with Gok Wan on another of his shows, *Miss Naked Beauty*. Klass has a similarly approachable and emotion-ally involved style of presenting as Wan, to the extent that she is often seen shedding tears along with the participants when they have their made-over selves revealed in the mirror scene. By the end of the first decade of the century, then, we find the 'ordinary' partici-pants being treated with more compassion, their emotional fragility perhaps symbolic of the economic fragility of the wider context.

To return to McRobbie's point about make-over shows featuring a legitimized form of class antagonism enacted at a corporeal level, I would suggest that this is not restricted to the postfeminist female competitiveness she discussed, but can be extended in a more acceptable way through the persona of Gok Wan, whose sexuality allows him to act with impunity, particularly as this is performed as part of his dual persona as professional stylist and gay best friend. Elsewhere, more overtly belligerent strategies are employed in interaction with fellow media professionals who are often characterized by an insincerely combative persona for our entertainment. Overall, we can see that the 'head girl' bossiness of early twenty-first century make-over shows has largely been replaced by the camp performance of the 'gay best friend' as personified by Gok Wan, while the underlying assumption remains that of women being constantly under surveillance with regard to their appearance.

Note on transcription conventions

(.) indicates pause of less than half a second.
(3) indicates pause of duration in seconds given in parenthesis.

Bibliography

Bartky, Sandra Lee (1990) *Femininity and Domination: Studies in the Phenomenology of Oppression*. London: Routledge.
Bonner, Frances (2003) *Ordinary Television: Analyzing Popular TV*. London: Sage.
Brown, Penelope and Stephen Levinson, (1978, 1987 edition) *Politeness: Some Universals in Language Use*. Cambridge: Cambridge University Press.
Davis, Glyn (2009) *Queer as Folk*. London: BFI.
Fraser, Kathryn (2007) ' "Now I am ready to tell how bodies are changed into different bodies ... " Ovid, *The Metamorphoses*', in Dana Heller (ed.) *Makeover Television: Realities Remodeled*. London: I. B. Tauris, pp. 177–192.
Gill, Rosalind (2007) *Gender and the Media*. Cambridge: Polity.
Heidegger, M. (1962) *Being and Time*. Oxford: Blackwell.
Higgins, Michael, Martin Montgomery, Angela Smith and Andrew Tolson (2012) 'Belligerent broadcasting and makeover television: Professional incivility in Ramsay's Kitchen Nightmares', *International Journal of Cultural Studies*, 15(5), pp. 501–518.
Kibbey, Ann (2005) *Theory of the Image: Capitalism, Contemporary Film and Women*. Bloomington, IN: Indiana University Press.
Lakoff, Robin Tolmach (2004) *Language and Woman's Place: Text and Commentaries*. Ed. Mary Bucholtz. New York: Oxford University Press.
Lewis, Tania (2002) 'Revealing the makeover show', *Journal of Media and Cultural Studies*, 22(4), pp. 441–446.

McLoughlin, Linda (2013) 'Bingo wings and muffin tops: Negotiating the exhibition of "imperfect" bodies in How to Look Good Naked', in Claire Nally and Angela Smith (eds) *Naked Exhibitionism: Gendered Performance and Public Exposure*. London: I. B. Tauris, pp. 165–189.

McRobbie, Angela (2009) *The Aftermath of Feminism: Gender, Culture and Social Change*. London: Sage.

McTear, M. (1985) *Children's Conversation*. Oxford: Blackwell.

Moseley, Rachel (2000) 'Makeover takeover on British television', *Screen*, 41(3), pp. 299–314.

Munt, Sally (2000) 'Shame/pride dichotomies in Queer as Folk', *Textual Practice*, 14(3), pp. 531–545.

Ouellette, Laurie and James Hay (2008) *Better Living Through Reality TV*. Malden, MA: Blackwell.

Palmer, Gareth (2004) ' "The New You": Class and transformation in lifestyle television', in Su Holmes and Deborah Jermyn (eds) *Understanding Reality Television*. Abingdon: Routledge, pp. 173–190.

Redden, Guy (2007) 'Makeover morality and consumer culture', in Dana Heller (ed.) *Makeover Television: Realities Remodeled*. London: I. B. Tauris, pp. 150–164.

Redden, Guy (2008) 'Economy and reflexivity in makeover television', *Journal of Media and Cultural Studies*, 22(4), pp. 458–494.

Richardson, Niall, Clarissa Smith and Angela Werndly (2013) *Studying Sexualities: Theories, Representations, Cultures*. Basingstoke: Palgrave Macmillan.

Richardson, Niall and Sadie Waring (2013) *Gender and Media*. Basingstoke: Palgrave Macmillan.

Sheldon, Amy (1990) 'Pickle fights: Gendered talk in preschool disputes', *Discourse Processes*, 12, pp. 5–31.

Shugart, Helene A. (2003) 'Reinventing privilege: The new (gay) man in contemporary popular media', *Critical Studies in Media Communication*, 20(1), pp. 67–91.

Smith, Angela (2010) 'Lifestyle television programmes and the construction of the expert host', *European Journal of Cultural Studies*, 13(2), pp. 191–205.

Smith, Angela (2013) 'From girl power to lady power?: Postfeminism and ladette to lady', in Claire Nally and Angela Smith (eds) *Naked Exhibitionism: Gendered Performance and Public Exposure*. London: I. B. Tauris, pp. 157–164.

Spelman, Elizabeth (1982) 'Woman as body: Ancient and contemporary views', *Feminist Studies*, 8(1), pp. 108–131.

Taylor, Lisa (2002) 'From ways of life to lifestyle: The "ordinari-ization" of British gardening lifestyle television', *European Journal of Communication*, 17(4), pp. 479–493.

Thornham, Sue and Tony Purvis (2005) *Television Drama: Theories and Identities*. Basingstoke: Palgrave Macmillan.

Weber, Brenda and Karen Tice (2009) 'Are you finally comfortable in your own skin?: The raced and classed imperatives for somatica/spiritual salvation in *The Swan*', *Genders*, 49.

4
Boredom and Reinvention for the Female Gaze Within Personal Fashion Blogs

Jennifer Anyan

> Metamodernism has been characterised as a pendulum swing between poles of enthusiasm and irony, hope and melancholy, naïveté and knowingness, empathy and apathy, wholeness and fragmentation.
>
> (Vermeulen and Akker, 2010)

Focusing on the work of three prolific personal fashion bloggers, themanrepeller (Leandra Medine), stylebubble (Susie Lau) and thestylerookie (Tavi Gevinson), within the context of metamodernism, this chapter will explore how the genre of personal fashion blogs are part of both the cause and potential solution to the characteristics of metamodernism. Boredom (with reference to Phillips's definition of it being connected to 'a wish for a desire' (1993, p. 71)), reflecting the pace of Web 2.0, twenty-first century fashion production and the emotional response to the pendulum swings of metamodernism is explored as a motivating state (supported by enabling technology) that has facilitated the activity of frequent reinvention by young western personal fashion bloggers in terms of the identity they express in the public online domain. This demonstration of fluctuating and flexible identity is manifested in using social media to control and export self-produced images that are constructed for the female rather than male gaze (Rocamora, 2011, p. 410).

With reference to postfeminism; the twenty-first century interactive media of the personal fashion blog reinforces a value system that prioritises qualities that are identified as feminine and preference a reciprocal relationship with the blog reader.

Introduction

Personal fashion blogs (PFBs) are a sub-genre of fashion blogs that consist of the author posting photographs of themselves (typically full-length), with the intention to document and show their style. The images are usually captioned with details of what the subject is wearing, including brands and sometimes price. Many PFBs also post accompanying text that discusses the outfit with reference to the occasion or event they wore it to, a new piece of clothing that the outfit has been built around, the visual references or inspiration for the ensemble and even the blogger's feelings at the time. Readers' comments classify a blog as social media – which is key to this article insofar as it discusses the authoring of feminine identity through social (interactive, as opposed to non-interactive media such as advertising, TV, film, editorial) media. The three PFBs focused on for the investigation within this paper are: themanrepeller, authored by Leandra Medine, stylebubble authored by Susanna Lau and thestylerookie by Tavi Gevinson.

The website Notes on Metamodernism documents examples of what authors and founders Vermeulen and Akker, as well as the other contributors to the site recognise as the cultural shift they call metamodernism (2010). This chapter also engages with the ideas that Giles Lipovetsky discusses in *Hypermodern Times* (2005), as well as some of the complexities of the modern fashion system and the impact of this on personal identity discussed in his earlier book *The Empire of Fashion* (1994). Of particular interest and relevance is what Lipovetsky refers to as 'Do-It-Yourself Enlightenment' (1994, p. 221) the notion that the individual is struggling within a society that on the one hand allows the individual to 'seek truth in themselves' while paradoxically, continually seeking the opinions and reassurances of others within an 'unstable environment with a frivolous economy of meaning' (1994, p. 222). Lipovetsky describes this as follows:

> people are more prepared to raise questions in the absence of preconceived answers, and they are more comfortable calling themselves into question as well.
>
> (Lipovetsky, 1994, p. 222)

The blog is a vehicle that allows the blogger to raise questions about the messages they are communicating through their appearance via the images they post of themselves. Through the comments function bloggers actively invite comment, criticism, praise – any form of feedback and response. Therefore the blog, as a tool, facilitates with ease the practice of asking questions that Lipovetsky (1994, p. 222) identifies as being characteristic of a society with a 'frivolous economy of meaning', a society in which meaning has few anchors and fluctuates. Lipovetsky's *The Empire of Fashion* was written almost 20 years ago, during what is recognized as the postmodern period; however, the conditions Lipovetsky refers to here, ' … in advanced democracies, ideological fanaticism is becoming extinct, traditions are coming undone; a passion for information is moving to the foreground' (1994, p. 223) that gave rise to people being 'more prepared to ask questions', are, if anything, heightened today.

Vermeulen and Akker's (2010) establishing statement on metamodernism being characterized as a pendulum swing between poles of enthusiasm and irony, hope and melancholy, naïvety and knowingness, empathy and apathy, wholeness and fragmentation from *Notes on Metamodernism* is particularly important in that this chapter argues that the societal characteristics described in this statement are also characteristics that are displayed by many personal fashion bloggers within their blog posts. The chapter will identify many of these metamodern characteristics within three personal fashion blogs and use these examples to demonstrate how the personal fashion blog is both a product of and a solution to the feelings experienced in metamodern society. The prefixes of 'post-', in relation to postfeminism, as well as 'meta-', in relation to metamodernism, are central to the personal fashion blogger, in that both words define an individual that is indefinite, precarious and fluctuating in their identity and image, and revels in this.

In describing metamodernism Vermeulen and Akker state:

> The ecosystem is severely disrupted, the financial system is increasingly uncontrollable, and the geo political structure has recently begun to appear as unstable as it has always been uneven. CEOs express their 'desire for change' at every interview and voice a heartfelt 'yes we can' at every photo op. New generations of artists increasingly abandon the aesthetics of deconstruction, parataxis

and pastiche in favour of aestho-ethical notions of reconstruction, myth and metataxis. These trends and tendencies can no longer be explained in terms of the postmodern. They express a (often guarded) hopefulness and (at times feigned) sincerity that hint at another structure of feeling, intimating another discourse.... (2010)

This description of a society that is unstable and has a desire for change (sometimes for change's sake) and is hopeful while simultaneously being cynical gives context to the twenty-first century Western world the personal fashion blogs discussed here are authored within.

Vermeulen and Akker then go on to describe metamodernism as:

characterised by the oscillation between a typically modern commitment and a markedly postmodern detachment... According to Greek-English Lexicon the prefix 'meta' refers to such notions as 'with', 'between', and 'beyond'. (2010)

They contend that metamodernism should be situated epistemologically *with* (post)modernism, ontologically *between* (post)modernism, and historically *beyond (*post)modernism. Rocamora (2013, p. 96) discusses in the essay 'Hypertextuality and remediation in fashion media' that the blogosphere is rhizomatic, not linear, or in other words, a number of co-existing plateaux and lines: places, people and centres that are connected through hyperlinks – connections to webpages that the reader can move between through clicking on text or image. It is the ideas of co-existence and the fluctuation between that are at the centre of the hypothesis explored in this chapter and that typify the metamodern characteristics of the PFB, in its use as a tool to constantly reshape the identity of the author, moving as a pendulum between poles.

Genz and Brabon suggest that the 'intersections of postmodernism and postfeminism cannot be conceived as harmonious union' (2009, p. 109), the contradiction between postmodernism and (post)feminism is marked as the difference between philosophical position and active position. However, Genz and Brabon do highlight that postmodern (post)feminism does reject the universal and singular conception of 'Woman' with emphasis on difference. With the foregrounding of this reading of postmodern (post)feminism in mind, metamodernism and postfeminism could be seen as more compatible from an existentialist standpoint in that the metamodern postfeminist embraces plurality and difference within one being and body. The metamodern individual in embracing a constant state of being in flux, is constantly repositioning and simultaneously referring to past as well as future. The PFBlogger embodies this position in their actions and choice of media being rhizomatic, previous blog posts are often referred to and hyperlinked to through the text, identity is reformed each time the blogger constructs a new image of themselves and posts their photograph. Whether consciously or not, PFBloggers are using social media for feminist objectives, they are the creators not just the creation, providing pluralistic visions of themselves. Susie Lau's post on 12 May 2013 titled 'UnTotal Look' exemplifies the pluralistic metamodern female approach to fashion and dress (Figure 4.1).

Lau uses the post to showcase various outfits and discuss the construction of these with reference to her refusal to wear Dior as a head-to-toe prescribed look. Lau highlights the fact that the blog allows her a greater freedom to experiment with dress than is allowed of stylists producing editorial for magazines who are required to comply with rules of the brands who advertise with them:

> It's a bit more of a wild wild West here in blogland where shoots aren't formal and advertiser credits aren't in existence (yet).
>
> (Lau, 12 May 2013)

In the post Lau discusses approaches to constructing outfits as the 'way we actually dress' and 'how our wardrobes are composed in reality'. This dialogue and the accompanying outfit images demonstrate a typically metamodern engagement with enthusiasm and irony as well as a postfeminist position that is concerned more overtly with an aesthetic discourse than creating an alluring image that is primarily designed to appeal to the male gaze.

Online social spaces

The rapid development of hardware, software and the Web 2.0 (with social media platforms being a part of this) has facilitated a new, democratic channel for women to use in shaping and

Figure 4.1 Susie Lau 'UnTotal Look'

communicating identity constructs for themselves in the twenty-first century. Digital systems have enabled blogs to become a new source of capital accumulation, through shifting the fashion economy towards immaterial commodities (Pham, 2013, p. 8). Affordable technology, including laptops, tablets and smartphones, as well as WiFi and roaming data services, enable social media to become an intrinsic part of everyday life. This space for reinvention would not have been possible without the supporting hardware, software and world wide networks that allow possibilities for quickly making and uploading new images, often 'selfies' (a term coined to describe a self portrait taken with a phone or camera at arms length, or for a more sophisticated version on a tripod with a timer or remote trigger), as well as the regular communication that builds online societies, often through a smartphone or tablet (used on the move) enabling conversation to be picked up at any moment.

thestylerookie.com blog was started by Tavi Gevinson in March 2008, a month before she turned 12. Born in 1996, living in Chicago, Illinois Gevinson's rise has been prolific:

> By the time Teen Vogue named her 'the luckiest 13-year-old on the planet,' in 2009, Ms. Gevinson had appeared on the cover of Pop magazine and starred in a video for Rodarte's Target line. Later, she was profiled by both The New Yorker and The New York Times Magazine. With her thick glasses and dyed blue-gray hair (Tavi was sometimes mistaken for an outré granny), she was a petite tastemaker.
>
> (Shulman, 2012)

Gevinson documented her style between the ages of 11 and 16 on the blog (Gevinson stopped posting regularly on the blog in 2012 and is now editor in chief for Rookie, an online teen magazine). Through the blog the reader sees Gevinson grow up, both physically and within all the roles she adopts – blogger, writer, stylist, taste-maker and social commentator. On thestylerookie Gevinson regularly documented not only outfits but often written posts as well as journal style posts, her mood boards and links to films, songs and websites that were cited as her style inspiration. Gevinson is refreshingly candid on the blog about the pressures, stresses and delights of being a teenage girl and it is this openness that is often discussed as being key to her success, along with her articulate communication and developed aesthetic, and has been celebrated by fashion community. Gevinson became a sensation in fashion circles because at the age of 12 she had established a blog with a credible voice and this technological tool allowed her the public space to assert her right to explore and express her developing identity and document it. thestylerookie gave Gevinson access to a world that would have been almost impossible for her to access before the invention of blogging and its supporting technology. Gevinson placed herself on a global platform that in turn transported her to the front row of a number of fashion shows for global brands and contributed editorial content to magazines including *Love* and *Pop*. Not only was Gevinson's image not mediated or produced, it was still developing (fluctuating in response to trends as well as her personal growth) and this was one reason for the blog's success. The success of the blog and its author shows the value the fashion media and its readers place upon the qualities that the blog and its author embody: metamodern fluctuations between enthusiasm and irony, hope and melancholy, naïvety and knowingness being particularly evident. The excerpt below demonstrates these poles within one blog post on 19 December 2009: Gevinson explains what could be identified as the 'swing' described by Vermeulen and Akker as 'random bursts' of inspiration throughout months of monotony. The phrase 'harder to hold on to' is also relevant to these metamodern characteristics in that it implies a struggle to grasp what she is looking for.

> Section 1.01: It feels like for months I've had random bursts of inspiration, but it's mostly just been monotonous, formulaic, or making sure I just barely have a decent outfit so I don't feel TOO lazy. Sure, there is inspiration that is more direct … a color scheme of a photo that you want to incorporate into outfit form; a character from a movie … but the inspiration to simply just be creative is harder to hold on to.

Gevinson's blog is more personal than that of Lau or Medine. The intentions of the blog (certainly in the first year) are not profit generating (in terms of either financial profit or gifts), she is genuine in her use of blog as journal and often writes openly about her feelings and the emotions that are influencing how she is forming her (fluid) identity. Gevinson, born in 1996, is a child of the metamodern world; she has grown up with a great range of technology available to her, therefore hyper-textuality and the nature of co-existence through the rhizomatic nature of new media is normal.

In his discussion of the culture of consumption Lipovetsky states:

> the logic of consumption and fashion has encouraged the emergence of an individual who is more the master [*sic*] and possessor of his [*sic*] own life, albeit basically unstable, without any deep-rooted attachments, and with personality and tastes that are always fluctuating.
>
> (2005, p. 23)

This could be the description of a personal fashion blogger; and the characteristics of being a 'master' of one's own life, without stability and with fluctuating tastes can be viewed in a positive light in terms of shifting or fluctuating metamodern identity. Alison Bancroft, in *Fashion and Psychoanalysis* argues: 'clothing deliberately sets out the insistent marginality of the body that renders selfhood precarious and unstable', (2012, p. 50). PFBs further facilitate the instability of identity and the premise that the identity of the self is constantly shifting through our response to our real world (face to face) and virtual world interactions with others. Furthermore, the self constructed for and portrayed through blogs and social media is not the same identity as actual self.

For the female gaze

The genre of the PFB or the 'what I wore today' blog is predominantly produced by and for women, thus the construction is centred around the female gaze (Rocamora, 2011, p. 410), offering an alternative to the historically dominant male gaze that established itself during the golden era of cinema and retained its hold in other areas of the media: TV, advertising and even to an extent fashion photography, the legacy of photographers such as Guy Bourdin and Helmut Newton, whose images presented a highly sexualized view of women, objectifying them for the male gaze. The purpose of the photograph, as well as the person who takes on the role of photographer in a PFB is what changes the emphasis from the male to the female gaze. Within the PFBs analysed for this chapter this emphasis on production for the female rather than the male gaze is due to the photographs often being self-portraits, constructed primarily to communicate style and details of the aesthetic of the outfit worn, with an additional agenda of engaging the reader of the blog in discussion about the outfit. Therefore, the photographer/author/model roles – all being undertaken by the blogger themselves (sometimes with assistance) – is active rather than passive, the emphasis is on clothing rather than the body. The technical construction of the images (poses, camera angle, crops, post production) is considered in order to prioritise showing the clothing rather than objectifying the woman. In addition, the journal or diary aspect of blogging, highlighted by Rocamora (2011, p. 411) and Sundar *et al.* (2007, p. 90) is a practice central to the process of identity construction, through enabling self-reflection.

Being bored

Firstly, it is important to acknowledge that boredom is not new and the psychological state of being bored is not an effect of metamodernism; there are many examples throughout cultural and social history of boredom being documented as a common condition, the nineteenth-century ennui being one. However, the psychological state of boredom does resonate with the pendulum swing described by Vermeulen and Akker (2010) and the instability described by Lipovetsky (2005, p. 23) in its elusiveness (Svendsen, 2005, p. 14); boredom is difficult to articulate and is fleeting. Svendsen also supposes that boredom and its cause is often intangible, with a close relationship to melancholy.

Boredom is more trivial than melancholy (Svendsen, 2005, p. 10). Svendsen also asserts that the world has become more boring, and that if boredom has increased it is because the overall meaning (of life) has decreased or even disappeared. Therefore it is logical that there is currently more experience of boredom in the world than ever before. Svendsen (2005, p. 26) attributes this to the fact that there are more 'social placebos' than ever before – Lipovetsky discusses hedonism (2005, p. 10) – both analogies refer to the idea of the continuous desire for a 'fast fix', a drug to make us feel better. This echoes the pace of new media image production and consumption as well as fashion production and consumption trends that have significantly speeded up in the last 20 years.

Boredom is not necessarily a negative emotion; in this instance boredom is explored as a motivating state, a mood that facilitates an active pursuit of change and the communication of that change through a personal fashion blog. Adam Phillips (1993, p. 71) purports that boredom is connected with the wish for a desire; in metamodern society this wish for desire can be linked to reinvention of the self and the recognition of that being successfully achieved, the sheer number of personal fashion blogs on the world wide web proves that this is a social priority for many people in the Western world, particularly young women. The blog format and functionality creates a platform for young women to stage this reinvention and pursue recognition for this. This format also allows the process to be facilitated at a pace the blogger controls, in that they control the frequency and timing of posting, with 'feedback' responses through the blog's comments section typically being within minutes or hours for bloggers such as those explored within this paper who have many global followers providing comments at all hours from all places.

The pace of what is 'interesting' – in fashion terms, the pace of changing trends – is well serviced by blogs and wider social media through constantly providing updates and new images. However, in allowing users of this technology to post and comment, to feedback almost instantly, the media itself is an active part of what facilitates the feelings of apathy, boredom and melancholy of people living in twenty-first century society. There is a sense of simultaneously wanting or hoping for, constantly, something new (having become accustomed to being saturated with images, updates and new products) as well as paradoxically feeling apathetic and bored with this continual state of moving on. It is this simultaneous contrast of feeling that characterises the metamodern condition – the pendulum swings between feelings of hope (for something new) and melancholy (about the need for this), empathy (understanding with this desire and lifestyle) and apathy (a lack of interest in continuing on this cycle). In the blogosphere nothing remains the same, there is always a new post or an update and there is very little time for enjoyment of or reflection upon one particular post or image.

Nevertheless, while simultaneously being part of the cause, new technology, new media and social media can also be a solution to the feelings generated by metamodern society, through allowing the user to assert some control over the media, either through authoring their own blog or commenting on someone else's. This is the key difference between social media and traditional media (in which we are bombarded with content but cannot interact with it). This meaning deficit (Svendsen, 2005, p. 29) produced through non-interactive forms of technology is being addressed through interactive forms of technology: for instance bloggers and blog readers are engaging with modern forms of social technology to address their meaning deficit. Blogs and the communities they create allow social groupings to develop. Through blogs the reader and author can identify with people who share their values, developing a personal value in this process of posting and feeding back for both the blog author and the (active) reader; the blogger is not isolated and is a protagonist rather than an object.

Objectification is removed, as the protagonist PFBlogger is active female, controlling both the image and the narrative. Therefore the PFB opposes the language of the dominant patriarchal order (highly established in non-interactive media (Mulvey, 2009, p. 16) such as Hollywood films, TV, editorial, photography and advertising). Valuing social grouping and dialogue exchange as well as the space for providing alternative (from the male patriarchy of non-interactive media) versions of female identity underlines the fact that some priorities in Western society have changed. The average age of marriage is later than previous generations (of those who choose to marry) and the average age for women to have children (if at all) continues to increase. According to the Office for National Statistics in 2011, 49% of women who gave birth in England and Wales were over 30 years old; the reasons attributed to this change are women spending more time in education and in building and valuing careers, and instability in relationships is also identified as an influencing factor. This shift in society has allowed women a greater amount of time in the twenty-first than in the twentieth century to build an identity that has broader anchor points than being a wife and mother. Society is also more accepting in the twenty-first century of lifestyles and identities that are not based on heterosexual roles, allowing for a greater number of ways in which females can identify with what is feminine.

In addition, there has been much academic analysis in recent years of the feminized labour market (Dwyer and Wyn, 2001; Harris, 2003).

It has been identified that it is typically female skills that are best suited to the economic growth areas of service, information and creative industries. As a result young females, such as Lau, Medine and Gevinson are part of a generation that not only has access to technology that is enabling their communication success, they live within a society that is showing a shift from male dominated to female dominated culture and industry (Rosin, 2010; Pham, 2013).

Stylebubble and the process of identification

stylebubble is not only a personal fashion blog, there are also feature articles and reviews. However, the personal fashion images are an important and consistent feature of the blog (in terms of why the blog is popular and in terms of Lau's professional identity); for the purpose of this article it is this content that will be the focus of discussion.

It is often difficult to identify and confirm exactly the identity and gender of the people commenting on blogs based on the names given and thumbnail identity images (depending on the settings of the blog to display these or not). However, to a certain extent it doesn't matter because the emphasis is on a female gaze, not necessarily the female gender of the person making the comment. The female gaze is identified here as a focus on the aesthetic and narrative of the outfit, as Rocamora and Bartlett state:

> ... the outfits shown on personal fashion blogs are often removed from a traditional feminine ideal. The bloggers often break with sartorial rules that can be perceived as part of the apparatus of submission of women to men. The very popular *stylebubble* in particular is the vector of an aesthetic situated outside of established cannons of femininity.
>
> (Rocamora and Bartlett, 2009, p. 110 cited in Rocamora, 2011, p. 420)

the desire to be the 'object' not have the object, in Lacanian terms relates to the mirror stage and categorises the process of identification rather than desire (Bowie, 1991, p. 30). It has been suggested by Fuss (1992, p. 714) in 'Fashion and the homospectatorial look', that fashion photography (which, given is a different genre but is related to this subject in terms of it being fashion imagery) looks to create not a heteronormative visual ideology but a femme-en-femme voyeurism that is inherently lesbian. This could be considered the case with PFBs but this is disputed here; the motive is not desire to 'have' the object (in the sense of the Lacanian object – the person, not the accessories or garments featured) in any erotic terms; it is a compulsive desire to engage with and be, through consumption – exemplifying metamodern impatience.

An example of this process of identification is the reader's response to a stylebubble post titled *Lady Lady!* from 2 January 2012. Below is Lau's intro followed by the reader response:

> Alongside those Merchant Archive finds are some old bits that I've resurrected after carefully clearing out the closet (five Ikea bags stuffed full of unwanted clothes remain for the taking . . .), a few sample sale buys and some Christmas/birthday gifts. Oh erm . . . and an accidental buy. I went into Liberty looking for Christmas cards and came out with a new season Dries van Noten skirt. I can only blame this Ab Fabby anecdote on the maddening period of merriment in exchange for swiping your plastic. Lady Lynn would not approve.

'Lydia' comments in response to this post:

> Jesus. Ok, first of all, that first outfit is probably my favourite [*sic*] I've ever seen you wear. Every layer and level of it is perfection. The other two are also amazing. I have had this awkward kimono in my closet for months that I just cannot seem to make work – you just inspired me to cut the sleeves off! Duh. And the ASOS sash top is just so cool.

> I totally watch Harry Potter around Christmas. Probably the most Christmasy movies ever that have nothing to do with Christmas.

> (*Lydia*)

There is camaraderie present, not only in the comments from 'Lydia' but in the way Lau introduces her posts/outfits: Lady Lynn will not approve . . . but the reader will. Lau's blog identity is performed *for* and identifies *with* the female gaze.

In terms of the construction of image for a male or female gaze it is pertinent to note here that the priority in many of the outfit posts is a need to communicate with some urgency to the viewer. The blog is a channel for a reciprocal relationship, the author is engaged with the reader and understands there is an expectation from the reader for the blogger to post regularly, both blogger and reader are implicit in building the relationship.

The photographs from the post *Stealing PJs*, posted on 28 March 2012, appear to have been shot quickly in whatever outside space was available to give natural light, as is often the case with images posted by Lau on stylebubble (Lau often shoots on the un-picturesque balcony of her London flat, in this case she is elsewhere, perhaps on a hotel balcony). The pyjamas are creased: Lau explains in the post that she ordered them immediately when she viewed them on the Topman website and wanted to share her 'find' as soon as possible after it arrived (Figure 4.2).

This post is referencing a series of previous posts on the blog that engage with the idea of wearing pyjamas as daywear. The regular reader will follow this stream of posts on the subject and engage with the exploration of pyjamas that Lau has been documenting over a two-year period on the blog, since 2010. There is an appreciation for the dialogue that the post engages with. None of the readers comment on the crassness of the imagery because a slick image isn't the priority here for the female gaze, it's the social connection through consumerism and it's the creation of an online society that appreciates and enjoys the same things. We connect with people we share interests with and the blog allows for people who enjoy the same tastes in clothing and fashion to share this, building a community of people who validate each other's taste in fashion. 'Betty' commented: 'ohh love it!!! think all bloggers shud go for pj's party and see who has the best LOL....' 'Manny' comments: 'How cool! You're making me want to go outside and get a pair of vintage PJs right now! P.S. I'm *loving* Betty's idea!:)'. These comments are an example of how stylebubble generates a community – not only are the readers engaging with Lau through their comments, they're also engaging in a dialogue with each other.

Themanrepeller and rejection of the male gaze

themanrepeller blog is authored by Leandra Medine who is based in New York. Medine is known through themanrepeller for

Figure 4.2 Susie Lau *Stealing PJs*

tongue-in-cheek, self-deprecating humour, accompanied by pictures in which she always looks well groomed, happy, sporting current trends. themanrepeller is a particularly interesting PFB in respect of reinvention for the female gaze and rejection of the male gaze in that it actively seeks to engage with fashion that challenges conventional feminine ideals of dress and makes light of this:

> **What is a man repeller?**
> **man·re·pell·er**[1] [mahn-ree-peller]
> *Noun*

outfitting oneself in a sartorially offensive way that will result in repelling members of the opposite sex. Such garments include but are not limited to harem pants, boyfriend jeans, overalls (see: *human repelling*), shoulder pads, full length jumpsuits, jewelry that resembles violent weaponry and clogs.

Verb (used without object),-pell·ing, -pell·ed.
to commit the act of repelling men:
Girl 1: What are you wearing to the party?
Girl 2: My sweet lime green drop crotch utility pants!
Girl 1: Oh, so we're man repelling tonight?
DISCLAIMER: The above conversation is not a dramatization, took place in this room 5 minutes ago.
Origin: 2009–2010; < *repellius* (ptp. of *repellia* to eliminate male attention), equiv. to L *repel-* (s. of *repellix*) unattractive, celibate, paris fashion week, M.C. Hammer + *-repel* – ler[1]

themanrepeller blog is more overt than both stylebubble and thestylerookie in being an online space that asserts construction of a feminine identity that is not built to appeal to the male gaze, and revels in frequently selecting items of clothing that could be considered challenging in terms of sartorial codes of what flatters the female body. This supports Rocamora's claim that:

> …on many personal fashion blogs, room is made for a female gaze, a gaze informed by the pleasures found in disrupting conventional visions of femininity, in experimenting with alternative

aesthetics, in dialoguing with ever shifting and unstable fashion rules

(2011, p. 420)

The engagement with an ever shifting, unstable dialogue of fashion trends also mirrors the metamodern characteristics of fluctuation between poles. PFBloggers revel in shifting identities and versions of femininity, thus embodying the metamodern mindset described by Vermeulen and Akker that is at the centre of this argument.

On feeling BLAH is a post from 21 March 2012 in which Medine dresses:

> for 'blah' days. It's a problem we all fall victim to, right? Blame it on the general notion of feeling uninspired or simply your body begging you to sit down and stop trying to socialize. Regardless, this morning when I woke up I looked out the window and saw hazy, grey, blah. Eureka! Here you have it: dressing for days you will inevitably feel like poopoo.

This post and the comment below from a reader provides an extreme, ironic and blatant example of how the viewers identify with wanting to become the object (blogger), evidencing again the process of reader identification with the blog author (Bowie, 1991, p. 30):

> Please don't tell me that's the entrance of where you live
> I might just kill you out of jealousy and steal your identity:)
> hey there's a topic for your book: blogreader kills blogger
>   and steals identity out of jealousy, the court says blogger
>   provoked it.:)
> Just kidding of course, couldn't be half as funny as you are:)
> Great blah outfit!
> greets
> Jennifer (*Jennifer D*)

Jennifer D projects herself into the shoes of the protagonist (Medine), to borrow a term from film.

Medine encourages readers of themanrepeller to engage in conversation with her through her tone in the Man Repeller guise (through the blog itself as well as the Twitter account and other social media) that is particularly casual and is geared towards opening a dialogue with the reader:

> Yesterday I tweeted a call for help that went like this: 'hey! Let's play a game called help me write my book, content suggestions welcome!'
>
> (Medine, 21 March 2013)

Post titles are often open invitations to answer a question or engage in dialogue on a particular topic, for example a post on 21 March 2013 is titled: 'I need your help!', demonstrating the importance of the interactive relationship with the blog reader.

Carrie Bradshaw's legacy

The character of Carrie Bradshaw in the HBO television series *Sex and the City* (running from 1998 to 2004) played by Sarah Jessica Parker became a style icon in the late 1990s and early 2000s. Her character was synonymous with a love for designer labels (which she couldn't afford) but also her independent spirit that was expressed fluently by stylist Patricia Field in the way she dressed the character. However, it is not only the 'Man Repeller' elements of the character's style (bandanas, men's y-fronts) that place her as a precursor to these bloggers – in particular Leandra Medine; Carrie Bradshaw has been dubbed the 'First female thinker in pop culture' by author and social critic Naomi Wolf (2009), and *Sex and the City* has been cited prolifically, sometimes controversially, as an example of postfeminism in popular culture. Wolf's claim that Bradshaw is the first female thinker in pop culture is disputable – this could be attributed to a number of people or characters – but the fact that the character is a writer, a columnist, is relevant to this argument in that the nature of the columnist is to update their readers regularly. The character of Carrie Bradshaw and her popularity with a female audience may give some insight into why PFBs that give personal opinion as well as an insight into the authors' life are so popular now. Carrie Bradshaw connected with a twenty-first century female audience through her dress, actions and dialogue. The dialogue was characterized by homosocial bonds (Gerhard, 2005, pp. 37–49) and much of the literature that characterises *Sex and the City* as postfeminist focuses on the friendship between the four main female characters (as well as their sexual independence). The aspect of the character Carrie Bradshaw that places her as a precursor to bloggers is the relationship and dialogue that is aimed at the viewer. Using a voice-over format to convey both an internal dialogue and narrate excerpts from the column Bradshaw writes for a fictional newspaper, Bradshaw addresses and asks questions of the viewer (as well as of herself). The difference between *Sex and the City* and the blogs is that the Bradshaw character is fictional and the media of television is non-interactive. However, the character of Carrie Bradshaw through both her penchant for reinvention through dress, advocating that buying and wearing fashion was an expression of independence and assertiveness, as well as the open communication, paved the way for the characteristics that are key to the success of many PFBs. Arthurs (2003, p. 87) in her essay '*Sex and the City* and consumerism: Remediating postfeminist drama' supports the view that feminine cultures of fashion and consumerism, a key element of *Sex and the City* as well as the PFBs discussed here 'have been considered a source of pleasure and power [for women] that is potentially resistant to male control'. In doing so, the postfeminist drama of *Sex and the City* and PFBs attempt to provide a method to overcome the division that second wave feminism constructs between feminism and femininity, the extent to which this works in practice, admittedly, varies. However, the three PFBs selected for discussion within this paper have been chosen particularly for this reason; each blog demonstrates the construction of a personal image that is engaged with a dialogue that is primarily about the aesthetic quality of fashion, rather than *predominantly* the body (as sexual object). Gill (2007) in attempting to define the characteristics of postfeminism, focuses her argument on understanding postfeminism as a distinctive sensibility that draws upon interrelated themes that include the notion of femininity as bodily property with an emphasis on self-surveillance, monitoring and empowerment that centre around sexual identity. This argument proposes that PFBs provide a platform that re-mediates other forms of media (TV such as *Sex and the City*, and glossy women's fashion magazines) but that allows young women to place emphasis on constructing a self-regarding identity whose primary preoccupation is not sexual identity; sexual identity is one aspect of these women and often not at the forefront of the images they construct (Figure 4.3).

Figure 4.3 Tavi Gevinson

Tavi Gevinson's post on 4 December 2010 demonstrates this and is primarily concerned with referencing and the narrative connected to characters and places rather than objectification of the body/person. Specific elements of the outfit are chosen to reference particular interests described here:

> Lady Miss Kier's ring game channeled through blue plastic thrifted belt and Goody daisy hairclips, the Edward Scissorhands (yes, this is a constant reference for me) neighborhood channeled through the hand-me-down skirt, Twiggy and clones sweater game channeled through sweater dress from PollySue's Vintage, and librarian cat channeled through purse I got as a gift.

The overall look created is knowingly ironic in creating an identity that communicates something of a woman much older than Gevinson herself in its aesthetic as well as a familiar character in the way that the artist Cindy Sherman has done through her artworks, such as the 1970s Film Stills series.

Like me

Engagement with identity and the formation of identity through social interaction on blogs is extended through the 'Like' feature on Facebook, we are identified through what we like and now most high fashion brands from Chanel to make-up brand Mac use this feature in their marketing. The 'Like' feature used to endorse brand preference, friends' status updates and photos reaffirms the 'Likers' identity and even existence through their preferences; I (actively) 'Like' therefore I am. In the Facebook design functionality, no distinction is made in the default 'newsfeed' we receive between our friends' status updates and the commercially driven content.

This chapter views social media such as Twitter, Facebook and tumblr as vehicles' that provide a platform to extend the practice of self-portrait or 'selfie' image posting on PFBs. The 'selfie' style of image posting that has been pioneered by PFBs is prolific within social media, evidencing that PFB imagery influences people who do not author PFBs in terms of making it a socially acceptable practice to post multiple images of themselves looking good. In the past, this practice might have been viewed as an act of vanity within certain cultures, and to some extent it still is by some. However, the prolific use of self-portraits through blogs and social media has normalized this practice and allowed a new space for viewing ourselves and placing images of ourselves in the public domain (for comment) that didn't exist before blogs and social media. In many ways the Internet allows for democracy through the ease with which anyone with access to a device with an Internet connection can communicate on a global platform. Specifically, through PFBs and the associated image posting through social media there is a greater range of imagery that depicts what is a fashionable female, allowing a space for dialogue that is about what women want to look like and how they wish to be identified. PFBs and social media have offered a space for women to control their own image within the public domain. For example, when media speculation broke that pop star Cheryl Cole's marriage to footballer Ashley Cole was in jeopardy in 2009, Cheryl Cole used Twitter to post a 'selfie' prominently displaying herself wearing her wedding ring, in a bid to reassert control over media speculation about her personal life and therefore identity (Johnson, 2009).

Post Notes, a feature of the image based blog site tumblr, are focused on documenting interaction between tumblr 'tumblelog' authors and their readers. This feature renders the post's 'notes' (any interaction with the post including reblogs and 'likes') on the author's permalink pages. This is the ultimate record in terms of documenting not only interaction but also the extent to which people respond to a tumblr post through 'liking' and reposting/reblogging. Post Notes evidence the value placed upon any interaction with posts within the social media sphere – even simple interaction, such as 'liking', reblogging and reposting, provides validation that the post is interesting. In commercial terms this is also important as users of blogging sites such as tumblr and blogger monitor user interaction through such tools in order to ascertain reader numbers – if they are high enough a blog may attract sponsorship or advertising and have the capacity to earn money through 'click-throughs' to sites selling product. tumblr Post Notes act as the glue for interaction, making a web of connections between tumblr posts and users – relating to Rocamora's (2013) description of web based media and the experience of using it as rhizomatic. Rhizomatic structure, a word used to describe complex root structures within horticulture, is a structure that by its nature can be difficult to negotiate and an experience that is difficult to navigate due to co-existing pages, dialogue and lines of enquiry can create a sense of confusion and flux for the user.

Apathy, melancholy and boredom

Alexander Forbes in his essay 'The Metamodern Mind-Set', published in the Berlin Art Journal writes:

> [the] geopolitical crisis and the economical crisis are affecting us. People from my generation always thought that we'd have better lives than our parents, and now we are realising that it's possible that we won't. Strangely however, when such generational disappointment could easily lead to an utterly postmodern response of 'fuck it, we'll fail anyhow,' the metamodern sensibility is quite the opposite. Out of loss in art, politics, bottom lines or otherwise, has come a resurgent hopefulness, or, even at times when the outlook isn't hopeful at all, a willingness to try. (2012)

Evidence of this melancholy – relating to the metamodern condition and the reaction to it, as well as the 'willingness to try' – is evidenced through the posting of self-portraits on PFBs. The practice of continually posting self-portraits actively demonstrates a desire to constantly renew, to constantly update the version of the self and to receive feedback on this. To constantly refer to a new set of references, or to an old set of references in a way that was different to yesterday. Consumerism is driven by the desire to constantly renew: the easiest way to renew our identity is to buy something new – be it an entirely new wardrobe of clothes or a new shade of lipstick. The fashion industry survives due to the notion that we constantly want what is different to what has gone before, the pendulum swing (Branning, 2010, p. 8) between short and long skirts, skinny and wide leg jeans, opulence and minimalism. The pace of the swing between trends is quicker than ever before in the twenty-first century in which production and distribution are faster and cheaper and catwalk shows are streamed live, increasing our desire and expectation that we should renew almost constantly.

In the following extract Lipovetsky discusses the reasons why he believes consumption has increased in the last 15 years:

> Through things what is being expressed in the final analysis, is a new relationship to personal existence, just as if people were afraid of getting bogged down, of not being ceaselessly provided with new sensations.
>
> (2005, p. 84)

This idea of not being 'bogged down' could be applied to the position of the PFB, or the person who uses social media to regularly post new images of themselves. There is a mood of restlessness, of constantly needing to move on to the next thing that is a reaction (that creates a sense of boredom and frustration) to the economic, social and cultural instability of metamodern times. Chitternden (2010, p. 14) discusses how the fashion blogs of teenage girls support a 'fluid notion of identity', using feedback from followers to form affinities and build what Bourdieu (1984, p. 249) termed social capital. Gevinson, in Chitternden's hypothesis of building social and cultural capital through a fashion blog, has been incredibly successful, as she has extended this beyond her own peer group into the fashion industry.

Conclusion

Personal fashion blogs have allowed a space for women to assert greater control over the construction of their image and identity within the public and global domain, re-mediating traditional and familiar forms of media to create a more feminized space. The pace of metamodern society, as well as its 'frivolous economy of meaning' (Lipovetsky, 1994, p. 222) encourages PFBloggers to engage with and revel in notions of identity that are fluid and fluctuating, without the latest reinvention negating the last, extending the boundaries of what can be identified as 'fashionable female'.

The popularity of the PFB can be related to the metamodern characteristics identified by Vermeulen and Akker (2010) and a feeling of boredom that the media itself perpetuates. PFBs allow bloggers to constantly renew and update, addressing the need created by metamodern society to harness control of the pendulum swings of these identified feelings. PFBs allow through their interactive nature a dialogue between blogger and (active) reader, creating a camaraderie driven social space that is on the whole supportive and encouraging, supporting Lipovetsky's theory of 'Do-It-Yourself Enlightenment' (1994, p. 221) being important for individuals to ask questions about their own identity, as well as engaging in postfeminist self-regarding discourse. The camaraderie driven virtual space of the PFB tends to preference female rather than male characteristics of gaze and the process of identification rather than desire. Facebook, Twitter and tumblr further extend potential for authoring and ownership of image reinvention within the public/virtual domain.

Bibliography

Arthurs, G. (2003) *Sex and the City and Consumer Culture: Remediating Postfeminist Drama in Feminist Media Studies 3:1*, pp. 83–98. Available online at: http://dx.doi.org/10.1080/1468077032000080149 (accessed 27 August 2013).

Bancroft, A. (2012) *Fashion and Psychoanalysis.* London: I. B. Tauris.

Bourdieu, P. (1984) *A Social Critique of the Judgement of Taste.* London: Routledge.

Brannon, E. (2010) *Fashion Forecasting*, 3rd Edition. New York: Fairchild.

Chitternden, T. (2010) 'Digital dressing up: Modelling female teen identity in the discursive spaces of the fashion blogosphere', *Journal of Youth Studies*, 13(4), pp. 505–520. Available online at: http://www.tandfonline.com/doi/full/10.1080/13676260903520902#.UbHpoYLBoTk (accessed 20 February 2013).

Dwyer, P. and Wyn, J. (2001) *Youth, Education and Risk: Facing the Future.* London: Routledge.

Forbes, A. (2012) *The Metamodern Mind-Set in Berlin Art Journal.* Available online at: http://www.berlinartjournal.com/issue/metamodern-mindset (accessed 28 March 2012).

Fuss, D. (1992) 'Fashion and the homospectatorial look', *Critical Inquiry*, 18(4), pp. 713–737. Available online at: http://www.jstor.org/stable/1343827 (accessed 29 May 2013).

Genz, S. and Brabon, B. (2009) *Postfeminism Cultural Texts and Theories.* Edinburgh: Edinburgh University Press.

Gerhard, J. (2005) 'Sex and the city: Carrie Bradshaw's Queer postfeminism', *Feminist Media Studies*, 5(1), pp. 37–49.

Gevinson, T. (2008–2013) *The Style Rookie.* Available online at: www.thestylerookie.com

Gill, R. (2007) *Postfeminist Media Culture Elements of a Sensibility.* London: Sage Publications. Available online at: ecs.sagepub.com (accessed 26 July 2013).

Harris, A. (2003) *Future Girl: Young Women in the Twenty-First Century*. New York and London: Routledge.

Johnson, C. (2009) *Diamonds Are Forever*. Available online at: http://www.dailymail.co.uk/tvshowbiz/article-1229495/Diamonds-forever-says-Cheryl-Cole-flashes-wedding-ring-Twitter.html (accessed 24 July 2013).

Lau, S, (2006–2013) *StyleBubble*. Available online at: www.stylebubble.co.uk.

Lipovetsky, G. (1994) *The Empire of Fashion – Dressing Modern Democracy*. New Jersey: Princeton University Press.

Lipovetsky, G. (2005) *Hypermodern Times*. Cambridge: Polity Press.

Medine, L. (2010–2013) *The Man Repeller*. Available online at: www.manrepeller.com.

Minh-Ha T. Pham (2013) 'Susie Bubble is a sign of the times', *The Embodiment of Success in the Web 2.0 Economy in Feminist Media Studies*, 13(2), pp. 245–267. Available online at: http://dx.doi.org/10.1080/14680777.2012.678076 (accessed 21 June 2013).

Mulvey, L. (2009) *Visual and Other Pleasures*, 2nd Edition. New York: Routledge.

Office for National Statistics (2011) *Live Births in England and Wales by Characteristics of Mother 1*, 2011. Available online at: http://www.ons.gov.uk/ons/rel/vsob1/characteristics-of-Mother-1-england-and-wales/2011/sb-characteristics-of-mother-1.htm (accessed 27 March 2013).

Phillips, A. (1993) *On Kissing, Tickling and Being Bored*. Cambridge, MA: Harvard University Press.

Phillips, A. (1994) *On Flirtation*. St Ives: Faber and Faber.

Rocamora, A. (2011) 'Screens as Mirrors', *Fashion Theory*, 15, pp. 407–424. Available online at: Berg Library of Fashion Theory (accessed 28 March 2012).

Rocamora, A. (2013) 'Hypertextuality and Remediation in Fashion Media', *Journalism Practice*, 6(1), pp. 92–106. Available online at: Taylor and Francis online.

Rosin, H. (2010) *New Data on the Rise of Women*, TED.com, December. Available online at: http://www.ted.com/talks/hanna_rosin_new_data_on_the_rise_of_women.html (accessed 21 June 2013).

Schulman, M. (2012) *The Oracle of Girl World*. *New York Times*. Available online at: http://www.nytimes.com/2012/07/29/fashion/tavi-gevinson-the-oracle-of-girl-world.html?pagewanted=all&_r=0 (accessed 27 March 2013).

Sundar, S., H. Hatfield Edwards, H. Yifeng Hu and C. Stavrositu (2007) 'Blogging for better health: Putting the "Public" back in public health', in M. Tremayne (ed.) *Blogging, Citizenship, and the Future of the Media*. New York: Routledge, pp. 83–97.

Svendsen, L. (2005) *A Philosophy of Boredom*. London: Reaktion Books.

Vermeulen, Timotheus, and va den Akker, Robin (2010) *Notes on Metamodernism*. Available online at: http://www.metamodernism.com/ (accessed 20 March 2011).

Wolf, N. (2009) 'Carrie Bradshaw: Icons of a Decade', *The Guardian*. Available online at: http://www.guardian.co.uk/world/2009/dec/22/carrie-bradshaw-icons-of-decade (accessed 27 March 2013).

5
In Full View: Involuntary Porn and the Postfeminist Rhetoric of Choice

Anne Burns

Introduction

> wow! i can't believe she sent the guy more nudes even after he
> posted her on here!
> Not the brightest...
> you got that right. but then again what would you expect from
> someone who posts nudes of themselves on their twitter too?
>
> (Comments, 7–9 April 2013, ugotposted.com)

This chapter analyses how the concept of 'choice' is deployed in the discourses on, and relating to, involuntary porn websites. These sites host images of (mostly) women engaged either in sexual activity with a partner or in sexualized self-presentations. The comments above demonstrate the focus on ridiculing the victims of involuntary porn, presenting the violation of their privacy as somehow their own fault. Although most images on these sites have been taken with the subject's consent,[1] the public sharing of such material is undertaken without their knowledge, either by an ex-partner (hence the alternative term 'revenge porn') or by someone hacking into under-protected web-based photo albums. The first site to host such images as a specific act of revenge, *Is Anyone Up?* (now closed), moved beyond the unauthorized sharing of personal material to combine images with the subject's personal information, such as Facebook, Twitter and LinkedIn profiles, as well as their workplace information. Numerous websites subsequently emulated this model, either for money (*Is Anybody Down?* charged women to remove their images) or for entertainment at humiliating others (*Pink Meth, You Got Posted, Texxxan* and *My Ex* among others).

Although humiliating women over their sexuality is by no means a new practice, the connectivity of the social media context, coupled with practices of data sharing, turns what might have previously been a limited and involved process of physically disseminating images into a straightforward and instantaneous act, but with far-reaching and unexpected consequences. Furthermore, the social media norm towards sharing relies on two factors: one, that data continues to be produced, and two, that data can be shared with relative ease. This creates both the material and the method for involuntary porn, enabling those with the right technological knowledge to obtain and distribute images that their owner might have otherwise have considered private.

The effects of the malicious sharing of intimate images has ranged from victims losing their reputation and job, to becoming targets of threats of sexual violence.[2] This is a gendered practice of discipline, where sexualized photographs are used by men to inflict shame and notoriety as means of degrading and punishing women. Furthermore, such sites perform a dual function; images of naked women provide both visual pleasure for their audiences, and the means for the aggressive condemnation of those depicted.

Theoretical approaches to 'choice'

In the public discourse around these sites, expressions of shock and condemnation exist alongside a strong sense of personal culpability, in which the woman depicted is held responsible for her predicament by virtue of it being her choice to engage in such photographic practices in the first place. It is this referencing of individual agency which I will be considering in this study, examining how the postfeminist rhetoric of 'choice' is utilized in distinctly un-feminist ways.

As Lahad describes, choice can be understood as a 'multivalent signifier' that reflects the shifting social contexts within which it is used (2013, p. 2). The ability to 'choose' one's own life path is a key component of how the prevailing culture conceives of the individual, with the ethos of modern society being that 'life is what you make it' (Beck-Gernsheim, 1996, p. 140; Rosenthal, 2005, p. ix). Rosenthal frames the ability to choose as an essential part of 'being modern', transforming not just how we live, but also 'how we think and who we are' (2005, p. 1). Exercising choice is part of the 'methodical conduct of life' where individuals are pressured to 'plan...make provision...control and optimise', in the form of making 'good choices' (Beck-Gernsheim, 1996, p. 142). But notions of such 'good choices' change with time and according to context, although the fact of 'having chosen' remains. Choice serves to 'haunt' the subject, where the freedom of 'choosing' is converted into a restriction to decisions made, emphasizing personal responsibility for the consequences (Rosenthal, 2005, p. 5).

Feminism and 'choice'

A core value of feminist thought is a woman's right to choose: on matters ranging from personal sexual preferences and family planning, to what career she seeks to pursue, choice is central. Probyn acknowledges this debt to feminism, in relation to the attainment of choice, and identifies the positions such discourses construct for women, in terms of the assumed 'natural' or 'good' choices (1993, pp. 278, 282, 284). In other contexts, as we shall see in relation to intimate photographs, some choices are taken out of the hands of the woman by virtue of being perceived as 'already made' (i.e. she chose to appear naked in photographs once, therefore appearing naked in other contexts is implied to be acceptable as a result of this choice) and with only one character to them (appearing naked in photographs is presented as 'universally bad', rather than part of a trusting relationship or exploration of sexuality) (Probyn, 1993, p. 285).

With the advent of postfeminism, choice became a signifier of a new, liberated sensibility, where individual tastes and lifestyles are celebrated in contrast to the perceived restriction of 'judgemental' feminisms past. But this 'choice feminism' (Hirschman, 2006), in which freedom is equated with the ability to make choices, underplays the pressures created by the social context and emphasizes women's self-determination (Wolf, 1994; Hirschman, 2006; Baumgardner and Richards, 2010). As Ferguson suggests, such principles can have distinctly un-feminist outcomes, when individual choice 'can be deployed to punish women who have "made" the wrong choices' (2010, p. 250). This demonstrates the dangers in advocating an unproblematic view of women's agency, as the 'theoretical attempts to rescue women from cultural dupedom' serve to elide the considerable pressures upon and penalties accorded to women's choices (Probyn, 1993, p. 281).

In the discourses I examine, choice is integral to both 'reactionary and utopic sets of discourses', in the sense that safety will be ensured if *you* are careful enough (Probyn, 1993, p. 292). The contradiction of choice, which emerges in relation to involuntary porn, is that despite the subjects suffering as a result of others' spiteful actions, it is asserted that the main source of fear should be yourself, and your own 'bad choices'. The deft way in which male oppression of women is re-articulated to become the fault of the victim is as impressive as it is alarming, and demonstrates the degree to which feminism needs to intervene in the representations of choice within public discourse (Probyn, 1993, p. 280).

Methods

This study considers how 'choice' operates in the discourses relating to involuntary porn sites. By examining the comments supplied by users on the sites themselves, as well as incorporating examples from other sources, I intend to explore how 'choice' is used to legitimate certain interpretations of the victims of involuntary porn. Additionally, to show the flexible interpretation of choice in this context, I will also discuss the site users' understanding of their own personal choice and opinion as enacted on the women they observe.

This study draws on the wider academic discourses surrounding contemporary user-generated media, relating to privacy, self-disclosure and the politics of visibility. Personal photographic practice serves as an intersection between gender normative expectations and the subjective interpretation and embodiment of feminist principles of empowerment. As such, the proscriptive and celebratory discourses surrounding women's use of photography are an important area for studying how patriarchal authority is enacted and contested.

Comments as research material

This study considers data collected from the comments section of 50 profiles that appeared on the involuntary porn sites *Pink Meth* and *You Got Posted*. As mentioned above, there are numerous such sites, and these two were chosen on the basis of availability (others having been shut down in the wake of legal action)[3] and for the presence of a comments facility at the bottom of each profile.

The ability to leave comments on websites is an integral feature of the contemporary, 'social' web, which foregrounds the making of connections and the easy sharing of viewpoints and media. Such practices of (unauthorized) sharing and connecting are integral to involuntary porn sites, and to the damage which they can do, but it is specifically the comments facility which will be examined here.

As reader responses to photographs, both male and female, the comments provide an insight into how such images are being consumed and interpreted, and how they fit within wider cultural understandings of gender, sexuality and 'choice'. Being self-presented, rather than elicited for the purposes of research, an analysis of user comments reveals the implicit attitudes of viewers, and their practices of judging and disciplining those they observe. But as Press and Livingstone point out, the advantage of using already existing data is balanced against the 'considerable undertaking' of finding and editing an 'overwhelming volume of material' which by nature is temporary and 'virtual' (2006, pp. 186, 188). Due to these practical constraints, this study will inevitably provide a partial perspective on the wider practices.

Studying involuntary porn websites

Feminist scholars have widely utilized the Internet as a resource for discourse analysis, ranging from considering 'performative shamelessness' (Dobson, 2013) and performativity (Van House, 2011) to the perception of the single woman (Lahad, 2013) and practices of sexual harassment (Herring, 1999, 2002; Lewis-Hasteley, 2011). Social media in general, and involuntary porn websites in particular, provide a rich environment for studying the discourses surrounding female sexuality, including those presupposed by the viewers' normative expectations of femininity. User comments provide a shifting, evolving record of opinion, perception and action, demonstrating how 'inequality plays out in the day-to-day realities of concrete lives and consciousnesses' (Press and Livingstone, 2006, p. 196) and forming an enormous resource for feminist researchers of gender discourse. The study of the discourses surrounding such sites, therefore, uncovers their features and identifies the 'ethical and cultural significance of a discursive mode which has the potential to pose serious ethical and material threats' (Jane, 2012, p. 2).

I shall be considering specifically how the comments on such sites represent a threat to feminist goals, by conceptualizing 'choice' as a tool for discipline, rather than a means for liberation. Therefore, instead of analysing the images themselves or the circumstances of their creation, this paper will take a Foucauldian approach by considering how their comments serve to legitimize the repression of women, and fit within a wider discourse of masculine authority. Within a patriarchal society, and particularly within a pornographic context, it is the voices of the male spectators, utilizing the postfeminist rhetoric of choice, who are imposing their readings on these photographs to suit their own objectives. Foucault's approach is particularly useful in this context as it exemplifies the relationship between knowledge/power and social conduct by describing the regulation of bodies (1977, 1978, 1980). In involuntary porn, the comments demonstrate the social-disciplinary implications of how such media forms are received, where women's bodies are subject to a regulatory voice not only relating to their appearance, but also to their conduct. The perceived 'obviousness' of the folly of choosing to engage in private sexual photography constitutes a discursive formation, which in turn sustains a 'regime of truth', where women are understood to be both imprudent and lascivious (Foucault, 2000; Thiel-Stern, 2009).

Findings – narratives of choice

I will be discussing three different aspects of 'choice' which appear in the comments on involuntary porn sites:

1. A *woman's 'choice'* to be photographed naked as a means for legitimating her humiliation.
2. The *consequences of 'choice'* which are presented as validated by her previous 'choice'
3. 'Choice' as exercised *by the viewer*, whether to share images in such a way as to sabotage the victim's social standing, or to express opinions over what he would wish to do to the woman, or how he views her.

A woman's choice

Empowerment as expressed through postfeminist discourses is the product of a woman's ability to choose, although this is limited by notions of what constitutes 'right' or 'desirable' choices. For example, as Atwood describes, a specific performance of 'sexy' femininity is valued, yet rather than empower women, this 'choice' to be sexy requires the internalization of an 'impossible and oppressive view of female sexuality', confined to a specific version of visible and nubile heterosexuality (2009, p. xix).

The supposed freedom of 'choice' implies that victims of involuntary porn are simply those that have made 'bad choices' in terms of their partner:

> The 'revenge porn' thing may be the hook that sells the story, but more important is the lesson about How Not to Find Healthy Relationships.
>
> (McCain, 2013)

or who have been victims of their own power-play:

> Let's not pretend that women don't prey on the 'weakness' in male sexuality, ie, its easy arousability for their own ends...Don't be naïve woman, life is lil bit more complicated than your tedious self pitying victim tirade.
>
> (Comment, 12 February 2013, clutchmagazine.com)[4]

A 'choice' in favour of (inadvertent) public nudity is a particularly volatile concept, which this comment identifies as automatically discrediting the subject:

> You put yourself naked into the public sphere. You deserve no sympathy.
>
> (Comment, 25 March 2013, clutchmagazine.com)[5]

Choice is an especially pertinent concept for women, with notions of a woman's 'right to choose' (in reproductive terms) or the presence or absence of choice (in terms of consent to sexual activity) remaining hotly contested, both legally and in terms of public discourse. The particular focus on sexual choices demonstrates the degree to which women's sexuality continues to be viewed with interest, and held to be especially significant of a person's subjectivity (Foucault, 1978). But the simplistic postfeminist equating of power with sexuality is unstable, as women's sexuality is still heavily proscribed, and vulnerable to being undermined through accusations of shamefulness and imprudence.

Shame

Shame which results from sexual ridicule is 'symbolically encoded with established meanings of femininity', making women particularly vulnerable to the reduction in status and self-esteem caused by such shaming (Cornell, 2000, p. 12). The negotiation around self-presentation to specifically avoid shame (Goffman, 1963) is particularly relevant in the social media context, where the imperative to be visibly 'authentic [and] hedonistic' exists in tandem with the requirement to 'maintain control of our sexual selves' and to restrict the visibility of the sexual self to certain audiences (Attwood, 2006, p. 92). The negotiation between the extremes of 'slut' and 'prude' produce 'contradictory worries' (Ringrose, 2011, p. 106), which requires continual self-monitoring to avoid the penalty of improper or undesirable forms of femininity.

Victim-blaming in the form of shaming is prevalent in the discourses surrounding involuntary porn, where sexualized images of young women become the means, and supposedly the justification, for shaming and insulting. Harassment is presented as a consequence of a 'bad choice' – a choice which implies the devalued and shameful subject position of the 'slut':

> Poor child... mabyee you shouldnt slut around... or trust ANY guys with your nude pics.
>
> (Comment, 22 May 2013, anonnews.org)[6]

Being perceived as a 'slut' is viewed as a personal failing and a lack of the required monitoring of the self, which is positioned as the route to power within postfeminist discourses of the individual (McRobbie, 2009). One commentator explains this, stating that:

> You know how to end this whole thing? Stop taking pictures of yourself spread eagled in front of a mirror and sending it to guys. Wow, problem solved.
>
> (Comment, 25 May 2013, clutchmagazine.com)[7]

Subjects are frequently chastised in comments for lacking the knowledge of adequate safeguards which would protect their photographs.

This is a logic that serves to blame the victim and their 'choices' rather than their aggressor. In this way, choice acts as a coercive and exclusionary force, where the exercising and display of such choices is endowed with value, and supports the creation of hierarchies. The commentators who criticize the victims of involuntary porn are placing themselves above them, being supposedly 'wiser' and more sensible. The comments below suggest that the choice to be photographed naked implies a lower status, by virtue of lacking self-respect, or parental guidance:

> I just don't get why a woman would allow herself to be photographed and filmed in the first place. Don't they have any self-respect?
>
> (Comment, 5 January 2013, huffingtonpost.com)[8]

> What they need to do is teach good morals. And then it's up to the kids to use them to stay out of things like this.
>
> (Comment, 28 May 2013, ugotposted.com)

Chastising the 'bad choices' made by the victims of involuntary porn serves to legitimate their abuse. It also implies that women should not only tolerate their denigration, but also see it as permissible, as we can see in a section of the *Pink Meth* website entitled 'Stories'. Here, the site elicits and displays narratives from the women whose images it hosts, warning other women not to make the same 'bad choices' they did. In return for this act of 'teaching sluts a lesson' in how to 'lock down their dirty flicks', the site claims it will remove those women's pictures, actively engaging the voices of fellow women to enact a mutual form of discipline on their peers (Foucault, 1977).

Locked in to choice

Choice, with its attendant associations of freedom and equality, enables a kind of lock-in, where the subject, by virtue of 'having chosen', is then firmly bound to their choices, as being in some way reflective of their self. This tethering of subject and choice embodies a new form of restriction, in which the circumstances of one's life are seen as the direct and logical result of one's own decisions:

> You are a victim of your own doing I'm afraid.
>
> (Comment, 25 April 2013, anonnews.org)[9]

> its YOUR FAULT for taking nude pictures of yourself in the first place...
>
> (Comment, 22 May 2013, anonnews.org)[10]

However, rather than being liberating, this conception of choice places the individual as entirely dependent on others' perception of one's choices, with little leeway allowed for circumstance or social context. The coercive power of 'choice' implies that women are now free from the limits and connotations of the past, being 'autonomous agents no longer constrained by any inequalities or power imbalances whatsoever' (Gill, 2007, p. 153). But in a climate where peer pressure, normative gender expectations and neoliberal discourses of individual responsibility overlap, a woman's sexualized self-performance becomes emblematic of both a claim for an empowered position, and a catalyst for its loss.

The 'choice' not to be a victim is presented as a 'simple' one:

> How about not allowing people take sex photos/videos of you in the first place?
>
> (Comment, 10 May 2013, theatlantic.com)[11]

> Keep your britches on while cameras are about, girls. You wouldn't be dealing with this if your [sic] weren't parading your stuff.
>
> (Comment, 26 January 2013, dailymail.com)[12]

> For individuals who would prefer not to be a revenge porn victim ...the advice will be simple: don't take nude photos or videos...And if you do, never share them with anyone else.
>
> (Goldman, 2013)

This is a reconfiguring of the feminist principle of autonomy, shifting from an empowered responsibility for the self, to a vulnerable position of limited choice yet bearing the consequences, and the blame. In comments relating to involuntary porn, the ownership of choice is presented as being empowered and feminist, even within a context which is explicitly anti-feminist, demonstrating the extent to which feminist principles have been distorted in such discourses. The simultaneous avowal and disavowal of feminism within such discourses is demonstrated by the use of feminism's challenge to passivity and reframing of 'sex as a source of strength and independence' to ultimately undermine feminism more generally (Attwood, 2011, p. 205).

The last comment, above, made by a lecturer in Internet law at Santa Clara University, California, reveals the extent to which even the legal standpoint on involuntary porn is one in which the victim has somehow brought such actions upon themselves. This notion of a lack of adequate self-protection, through carelessness or through ignorance, assumes that it is possible to either know another's intentions in advance, or know the ways in which technology can be exploited. The latter in particular poses a problem for many users, as the Internet is often 'experienced as unfamiliar, confusing [and] easier to get wrong than right' (Press and Livingstone, 2006, p. 190).

Goldman suggests that new laws are not needed as much as a change in the 'social mores about online nude/sexual depictions' (forbes.com, 28 January 2013). By this rationale, until society changes its perspective on women's sexuality, ending the stigma associated with involuntary porn, women are effectively on their own, and are responsible for their own protection. The centrality of individual culpability means that 'choice' serves to direct blame at the victims, where one choice made in the past implies a wealth of additional consequences. One woman's threat to go to the police receives a response that references this institutional indifference:

> Haha try and prove it bitch ... so many girls here have gone to the police thinking they might do something and their pictures are stil up here lol.
>
> (Comment, 25 May 2013, ugotposted.com)

The conception of choice as inherently 'bad' or 'good' has little in the way of nuance, which is reflected in the implication that participating in sexualized photography privately also entails their public availability:

> [If] you're cool with nude photos spreading on the Internet ... then by all means, break out the camera in the bedroom.
>
> (Hill, 2009)

Franks identifies the ludicrously proscriptive basis for this standpoint, characterizing it as advising women to:

> Never ... take off your clothes in any context where anybody could possibly ever have a camera.
>
> (Quoted in Cochrane, 2012)

Franks identifies the popular discourse's reframing of responsible behaviour as a form of paranoia, where making the 'right choice' implies trusting no-one, and where forgoing a level of intimacy is supposedly in one's own best interests. This 'worst case scenario' approach to making choices is based on being always prepared for the most extreme outcome. As a type of victim-blaming, this sense of harassment being 'disturbing but predictable' (James, 2013) implies that the victim simply did not prepare adequately for an expected eventuality. Social inequalities are thereby reflected back onto the individual, so that a cultural norm for slut-shaming is reframed as correcting the subjects' own flaws and ignorance (Lahad, 2013, p. 13).

The consequences of 'choice'

Involuntary porn sites are based on a principle of sexualizing non-compliance, in which the attraction for viewers is that they make visible something that would normally be hidden (Cochrane, 2012). Scopophilia is the 'love of looking' and includes the sexual pleasure involved in seeing another person, especially where the sense of separation engendered by the photograph gives the 'illusion of looking in on a private world' (Mulvey, 1975, p. 9). Here, the voyeuristic gaze extends this enjoyment of looking to convey a particular sort of viewing pleasure, predicated on having power over the subject observed.

Voyeurism and punishment

Taken to an extreme, such erotic practices of looking have a sadistic character, where sexual satisfaction can only be obtained through a controlling and voyeuristic gaze that fundamentally disempowers those who are looked at (Mulvey, 1975, p. 9). Conversely, the lack of such a sense of control, by virtue of the subject's disinterest in being viewed, is a source of disappointment for some users:

> I thought this site was to post nudes that no one wanted on the internet? Obviously, if you're walking around in public naked, you don't give a shit, and that takes the fun out of why I come here.
>
> (Comment, 21 February 2013, ugotposted.com)

Generally, in the context of involuntary porn, the unauthorized over-riding of someone else's privacy is given a sense of legitimacy, in that 'they were asking for it' by virtue of their earlier 'choice'. This reveals an interesting approach to consent, in that it can be concep-tualized to suit the needs of the viewer, depending on whether they wish to obtain pleasure from transgression, or satisfaction through punishment, or both:

> We obviously don't give a fuck about morals or how the girl feels. We're in this for our own satisfaction. The satisfaction that comes from having sex is entirely different than the sat-isfaction that comes from seeing someone humiliated on the internet.
>
> (Comment, 25 May 2013, ugotposted.com)

The expectation of seeing sexual images, coupled with the desire to chastise the women depicted, mirrors the sadistic gaze that Mulvey describes in relation to narrative cinema (1975). Investiga-tion of the woman, followed by her discipline, forms a narrative arc for Mulvey, which she identifies as referencing Freud's cas-tration complex. The 'threat' posed symbolically by the woman is negated by her observation and correction, 'helping' her to see the error of her ways, as a result of the intervention of a disciplinary male.

The investigation seeks to ascertain her guilt, and thereby her need to be punished or saved (or both). For Mulvey, this has clear sadis-tic overtones, whereby a certain pleasure lies in attributing guilt as a means for 'asserting control and subjecting the guilty person to punishment or forgiveness' (1975, p. 14). This forms clear parallels with the practices of looking, assessing and punishing characteristic of involuntary porn sites, in which the spectator imposes their own story upon the subject (focused, I argue, on the notion of 'choice') as part of a sadistic will to change 'another person' through a 'battle of will and strength' (Mulvey, 1975, p. 14). The battles of wills on such sites, however, are clearly mismatched in favour of the specta-tor, who, as the invisible investigator, is in a position of mastery and domination.

The culmination of the narrative Mulvey describes in relation to voyeuristic scopophilia, in which the woman receives a punishment as a resolution of her 'guilt', is exemplified by viewers expressing a sense of women 'deserving' being publicly 'outed' in this way:

> good she got posted hahah. Viewing her photos and one of her caps is 'hope this is my first picture to get 100 likes' what a dumb attention seeking cunt.
>
> (Comment, 28 May 2013, ugotposted.com)

Users often defend such practices as teaching women a valuable lesson, in which 'threats and/or fantasies of violent sex acts ... are often framed as "correctives"' (Jane, 2012, p. 3). 'Deserving' punishment is presented as a consequence of seeking male attention:

> Yup, hate ugly bitches that want attention.
>
> (Comment, 27 May 2013, ugotposted.com)

> it doesn't matter why you took the pictures.... You were looking for attention and admiration, now you've at least gotten attention. You're nothing but a picture and a name, an object if you will. No one cares how you feel, what you think, what you do, or what your intentions are.
>
> (Comment, 3 February 2013, pinkmeth.doxing.me)

Even expressions of dismay at the content of some images can still reference this overall theme of punishment:

> That's not cool ... She's crying ... don't get me wrong some of these girls deserve to be punished, but putting up crying pics? ... Not cool.
>
> (Comments, 27 May 2013, ugotposted.com)

Which receives the reply:

> I can only get off if they cry.
>
> (Comment, 27 May 2013, ugotposted.com)

After a woman expresses distress at her images being uploaded, she receives a number of replies that chastise her, and accuse her of being unfit for her job. Her explanation that the photographs date from 'a lifetime ago' and a 'different lifestyle' fails to register, as within this context being photographed naked is a choice which marks one permanently:

> PLEASE remove these asap!... they are 6 years old which is a life-time ago for me when I was living a different lifestyle... I got kids, family, job, please have some compassion and remove them.
>> (Comment, 27 May 2013, ugotposted.com)

> So you regularly went around naked in some kinky scene, and 6 years later are the director of some children's ministry at a church? You are fucking weird. I would NEVER want you to instruct my kids.
>> (Comment, 28 May 2013, ugotposted.com)

> Wtf are you doing working around kids when you think its fine to show your tits and ass and pussy like its nothing... Can't feel bad for you... (Your going to HELL)
>> (Comment, 29 May 2013, ugotposted.com)

Punishment extends beyond display on involuntary porn sites themselves, as some users describe taking pleasure in sabotaging the women's social and working relationships by reposting intimate images on other public sites. One of the most alarming aspects of *Is Anyone Up?* and its imitators was that it allowed uploaders of photographs to include information regarding the victim's social media accounts, workplace and full name.[13] Exploiting the connectivity and openness of social media to their advantage, and furthering their 'investigation' of the 'deviant' female to find 'proof' of her guilt, such users deliberately transgress the borders separating their victim's private and public life, often with the vocal support of observers:

> her facebook is open/public, tempted to reupload and post this shit in her facebook

> do it :p.
>> (Comments, 28 May 2013, ugotposted.com)

> 100 Points to the sob that links her photo to her employeer's [*sic*] facebook

Dare me to do it.

(Comments, 29 May 2013, ugotposted.com)

Destabilizing a woman's career seems to be the aim for some users, who take pleasure in their power over women, and capacity to cause havoc:

She's a complete slut. Not good for career. She's really fucked.
(Comment, 3 February 2013, pinkmeth.doxing.me)

I'd hire her. But I wouldn't pay her. Good luck getting a job ever.
(Comment, 3 February 2013, pinkmeth.doxing.me)

One *Pink Meth* user uploaded a screenshot of a Facebook profile of a woman's workplace, which now – as a result of his intervention – featured an image of her engaged in a sexual act. Such acts of 'punishment' constitute what Jane calls 'e-bile', which is characterized by a sense of competition in which 'players joust to produce the most creative venom, break the largest number of taboos, and elicit the largest emotional response in targets' (2012, p. 4).

Punishment and sabotage demonstrate the fallacy underlying the postfeminist connection of sexual expression with empowerment, as such knowledge about an individual has markedly different values and effects depending on context and audience. Here, we also see the legacy of postfeminism's prioritizing of 'choice', as it serves to legitimize the viewers' desire to chastise women for their 'shameful' behaviour and 'bad choices'. In this way, although the language of choice exhorts women to be 'independent and maintain themselves', it also provides the context for their humiliation and disempowerment (Beck-Gernsheim, 1996, p. 146). This can be seen as a backlash against women's independence (Faludi, 1991), where by virtue of undermining a woman's social mobility in response to her 'bad choices', the logic of 'choice' in fact *increases* her dependence upon men, and her vulnerability to the opinions of and uses they have for her.

The viewer's choice

In contrast to the women who have had their choice overridden, the voice of the viewer is to be found clearly expressing its own choices and intentions, whether in terms of rejection:

I'd rather take a drinking glass, break it up into tiny shards, then rub my cock into those glass shards repeatedly than to poke this nasty skank.

> (Comment, 21 May 2013, ugotposted.com)

or enthusiastic sexual engagement:

Would rape.

> (Comment, 29 May 2013, ugotposted.com)

Id fuck the shit out of this sexy bitch.

> (Comment, 22 May 2013, ugotposted.com)

Despite the blame and accusations levelled at the women who appear on involuntary porn sites, there is also a strong sense – unsurprisingly – that the visitors to the site are only criticizing the women's choices in order to denigrate them, rather than truly calling for them to stop such behaviour and 'protect' themselves. The dual sense of criticizing and demanding sexualized photographs can be observed in the prevalence of comments enjoying the images:

One of the best bodies I've seen on here props to you.

> (Comment, 27 May 2013, ugotposted.com)

as well as others which loudly bemoan the lack of sufficient flesh on show:

show your tits biatch.

> (Comment, 28 May 2013, ugotposted.com)

you you stupid whore get naked or get away.

> (Comment, 21 May 2013, ugotposted.com)

Additionally, the interpretation of the 'choice' to appear naked is heavily dependent upon whether the woman is found desirable by the viewer:

Why is it that the big ugly broads have tons of pics and the hot girls only have 1 or 2. Fuck this shit.

> (Comment, 29 May 2013, ugotposted.com)

20 year old pussy = community pussy

50 year old pussy = keep that shit to YOSELF
                              (Comment, 7 March 2013, ugotposted.com)

As these comments suggest, beneath the veneer of women's autonomy implied by choice, the old sexual dynamic and devalued female
subject position remains intact. Women here are expected to fulfil a
sexual function for the viewers, according to their terms, and it is the
failure to meet these needs which causes scorn. The woman's choice
to remain clothed does not protect her from criticism, but merely
exposes her to a different kind. Franks identifies both instances of
criticism, at the clothed or unclothed woman, as a rage at women
being sexual on their own terms:

> We're perfectly fine with women being sexual, as long as they are
> objects and they're passive, and we can turn them on, turn them
> off, download them, delete them … But as soon as it's women who
> want to have any kind of exclusionary rights about their inti-
> macy, we hate that. We say, 'No, we're going to make a whore out
> of you.'
>   (Quoted in Cochrane, 2012)

The sense of viewer entitlement demonstrates that whatever the
choice made by the woman, the very act of choosing still serves as a
trigger for disciplinary power, rather than a means for liberation, as it
takes place within a context of patriarchal expectations and standards
(McRobbie, 2009).

Beyond questions of consent, there is a sense here of women's
bodies being public property for enjoyment. The practice of taking
'creepshots' (candid and sexualized photographs of women in public)
also constitutes a form of involuntary pornography, as it fetishizes
'non-consensual sexual activity with women who either you don't
have any access to, or have been denied future access to' (Franks,
quoted in Cochrane, 2012). The deliberate overriding of a woman's
choice not to be depicted sexually and publicly is, in Franks' terms,
a 'product of rage and entitlement' (quoted in Cochrane, 2012). One
creepshots site describes a view of the world that revolves entirely
around the viewer and their needs, rather than the choices made by
others:

There are creeportunities everywhere: durring [*sic*] your commute, shopping, coffee shops, office...or just even walking down the street! How about creeping your wife?

(Comment, 23 February 2013, creepshots.com)

As suggested above, and below, even intimates are vulnerable to this predatory attention, in which the absence of choice is actively desired:

GF got hammered and passed out in bed. Anon BF decides to grab a camera and creep some sexy pics. Even rolled her over to get the boobs, cuz we all know you can never leave out the boobs.

(Comment, 26 April 2013, creepshots.com)

If a woman protests and exercises her 'choice' not to be depicted on the site, the reaction she receives mixes a sense of expectation that this attention would be welcome, with a degree of blame for 'eliciting' such attention in the first place (by virtue of what she was wearing):

You can admire the fact that there is something about you sexy enough that somebody wanted to creep you...If however, you wore something sexy, tight or revealing and are shocked, ashamed, belittled or embarrassed that you were creeped and posted on here, then contact us.... Your request will be reviewed and if it is found legitimate, the picture will be removed.

Again, the choice of the woman to be viewed as she wishes (sexual/not-sexual, visible/not-visible) ultimately depends on the viewer, and whether he finds her request 'legitimate' or her image satisfying. Furthermore, it positions women's non-consensual sexuality as positive and 'un-slutty', in opposition to the debased connotations of a woman's 'choice' to be sexual.

Desire and repulsion

The aggression levelled at the women on involuntary porn sites hinges on the duality of the notion of 'choice'. On the one hand, the women are berated for their 'sluttishness' and their 'stupidity' for being photographed in this manner. On the other hand, some comments directly concern the overriding of women's choices by virtue of making their images more widely visible. The contradictory nature of the demands and expectations of women is clear, as despite numerous commentators suggesting that these images shouldn't exist at all, they see no problem in sharing and duplicating them once they do exist. This implies that, like the images themselves, the women depicted have the quality of objects which can be accessed, shared and owned at will:

> I am saving these pictures on my flash drive of girls I like
> (Comment, 21 May 2013, ugotposted.com)

Making the personal information of another available against their wishes is an aggressive act no matter what the circumstances, but there is something particularly spiteful about the deeply gendered symbolic violence that is contained within the sharing of private sexual images of women. These commenters know the degree to which this is distressing their victim, and take distinct pleasure in this:

> I saved all of your pics. I even posted them on other sites. Your welcome.
> (Comment, 25 May 2013, ugotposted.com)

> Also saved and reposted... Bitch must deserve it. You're everywhere now, people will search ur name on Google and see these.
> (Comment, 25 May 2013, ugotposted.com)

The gendered nature of this violence becomes apparent in the degree to which abuse combines sexualized imagery with expressions of disdain:

> Hahaha I just jacked off to your ugly fucking tits bitch! ... Btw there's nothing you can do now anytime anyone ever does a pic search on google they'll see your nasty pussy.
> (Comment, 20 May 2013, ugotposted.com)

Desire and repulsion appear contradictory yet intertwined, demonstrating the co-existence of practices of shaming and consuming the women they view:

I want to party with these whores.
>   (Comment, 27 May 2013, ugotposted.com)

I'm trying to decide if that pussy makes me sick, or horny as fuck.
Both I think.
>   (Comment, 22 May 2013, ugotposted.com)

I'd nail her but I'd want a few drinks first.
>   (Comment, 21 May 2013, ugotposted.com)

For many users, the entertainment value or sexual pleasure seems to lie in relation to the devaluing and humiliation of the women depicted. The conflation of desire and disdain is captured particularly succinctly in the comment below, where the words 'hate' and 'masturbate' are themselves conjoined:

> nothing like a nice hard hatebate and bustin a hatenut over some fucking bitch's faces and tits.
>   (Comment, 20 May 2013, ugotposted.com)

In this manner, the viewer can express desire for the woman depicted but within a context of firmly disempowering her. These conflicting sentiments reference a discourse on sexuality in which contradictions abound, where debasement and humiliation exist as sources of sexual satisfaction.

Conclusion

In this chapter I have explored three major themes relating to choice in the involuntary porn context, relating to: a woman's choice to be photographed naked and how this is perceived and used against her; the deliberate overriding of the victim's choice in making such images public; and the exercising of choice through the assessing voice of the viewer. In this way, choice can be either accorded to or denied to the woman depicted, enabling the viewer to act as they wish, while maintaining a sense of justification.

I have shown how engaging in private sexualized photographic practice can be used to form a hierarchy, separating those who 'do' from those who 'don't', and positioning those who look in a superior position relative to those who are seen. The comments reflect the sense of satisfaction and visual pleasure expressed by spectators, where sexual fantasies are described as a means to both enjoy and correct the women they survey. The sense that involuntary porn victims have 'brought it on themselves' serves to trivialize their suffering, encouraging them to 'lighten and/or harden up' rather than receive support (Jane, 2012, p. 9). Underplaying and undermining the experience of victims also serves to excuse the actions of the online aggressors, explaining it as 'to be expected' or even something to be defended and celebrated (Jane, 2012, p. 7).

Involuntary porn sites demonstrate the point at which feminist and anti-feminist voices overlap, both exhorting the importance of 'choice', but with very different objectives. Elements of postfeminist rhetoric occur throughout the discourses surrounding these websites, stressing individual responsibility, the role of 'free' choice and the need to self-monitor the body. The cherished postfeminist concept of 'sexiness' continues to be celebrated in this context, but viewed as a valued commodity, which the owner should 'choose' to guard and share with discretion. Anti-feminist conceptions of choice distort the postfeminist language of self-determination and demonstrate its vulnerability, undermining the sense in which 'choosing' to be sexy or wild is seen as positive, and instead using it as a means for expressing misogynistic views of women.

This undermines the postfeminist discourses' promotion of 'choosing' sexual empowerment, as it renders the female subjects in the profoundly disadvantaged position of being 'tawdry, tarty' and debased (Levy, 2005, p. 5). Rather than enacting a proud or independent sexuality, the victims of involuntary porn are stigmatized and vulnerable. These subjects have not enacted a 'choice' to be viewed in this way, yet their sexual expressions are used as evidence of a devalued subjectivity. The female subject is therefore left in a difficult position, made vulnerable by the collision of postfeminist conceptions of 'choice' with wider social norms and prejudices, and attributed with the power to 'choose' only to have it used against her, or overridden.

Limitations of the study and suggestions for further research

This study has been limited to an analysis of the comments on, or relating to, involuntary porn websites, and as such has not considered issues of participant motivation (for taking photographs) and positive instances of sexualized self-photography, as well as the wider context of social media practice or the use of pornography.

Further research is needed to explore the resistant voices which are to be found on these sites, both male and female, as well as the emergent legal measures taken to address these practices. Another area of interest would be a comparison between how men's and women's images are received on such sites – although involuntary porn is not restricted to women, male victims appear much less frequently. Also, I did not have the space here to consider the presence of underage girls on the sites I examined, as several comments discussed the subject's age, seemingly with an awareness of the legal implications.

Notes

1. Except those which feature women asleep or in public. Such 'creepshots' specifically seek to capture sexualized photographs of women unawares.
2. http://www.endrevengeporn.com/victims-speak-up.html
3. Since data was collected, *Pink Meth* has also closed, although the name appears to be shared by other, similar operations.
4. http://www.clutchmagonline.com/2013/02/revenge-porn-a-dish-best-served-by-a-disgruntled-ex/comment-page-1/#comments
5. http://www.clutchmagonline.com/2013/02/revenge-porn-a-dish-best-served-by-a-disgruntled-ex/
6. http://anonnews.org/forum/post/7243
7. http://www.clutchmagonline.com/2013/02/revenge-porn-a-dish-best-served-by-a-disgruntled-ex/comment-page-8/#comments
8. http://www.huffingtonpost.com/2013/05/01/revenge-porn_n_3194752.html
9. http://anonnews.org/forum/post/31118
10. http://anonnews.org/forum/post/7243
11. http://www.theatlantic.com/technology/archive/2013/05/how-to-fight-revenge-porn/275759/
12. http://www.dailymail.co.uk/news/article-2268476/Ex-plicit-revenge-porn-site-allowed-jilted-lovers-anonymously-post-revealing-pics-girlfriends-facing-class-action-suit.html
13. Alarmingly, Hunter Moore's new website, to replace the defunct *Is Anyone Up?* will apparently feature the additional field of 'address'. He acknowledges that this facility is 'scary as shit': http://betabeat.com/2012/11/hunter-moores-scary-as-shit-revenge-porn-site-will-map-submitted-photos-to-peoples-addresses/

Bibliography

Attwood, Feona. (2006) 'Sexed up: Theorizing the sexualization of culture', *Sexualities*, 9(1), pp. 77–94.

Attwood, Feona. (2011) 'Through the looking glass? Sexual agency and subjectification online', in Ros Gill and Christina Scharff, (eds) *New Femininities: Postfeminism, Neoliberalism and Subjectivity.* London: Palgrave Macmillan. pp. 203–214

Baumgardner, Jennifer and Richards, Amy. (2000, 2010) *Manifesta: Young Women, Feminism and the Future.* New York: Farrar, Strauss and Giroux.

Beck-Gernsheim, Elisabeth. (1996) 'Life as a planning project', in Szerszynski, Bronislaw; Lash, Scott and Wynne, Brian (eds) *Risk, Environment and Modernity: Towards a New Ecology.* London: Sage, pp. 139–153.

Cochrane, Kira (2012) 'Creepshots and revenge porn: How paparazzi culture affects women', *The Guardian*, 22 September. Available online at: http://www.guardian.co.uk/culture/2012/sep/22/creepshots-revenge-porn-paparazzi-women (accessed 23 May 2013).

Cornell, Drucilla. (ed.) (2000) *Feminism and Pornography.* Oxford: Oxford University Press.

Creepshots (2013) Available online at: http://creepshots.com/ and http://creepshots.tumblr.com/ (accessed 23 May 2013)

Dobson, Amy Shields (2013) 'Laddishness online: The possible significations and significance of "performative shamelessness" for young women in the post-feminist context', *Cultural Studies,* 28(1), pp. 142–164

Faludi, Susan (1991) *Backlash: The Undeclared War Against American Women.* New York: Crown.

Ferguson, Michaele L. (2010) 'Choice feminism and the fear of politics', *Perspectives on Politics*, 8, pp. 247–253.

Foucault, Michel. (1977) *Discipline and Punish.* London: Tavistock.

Foucault, Michel. (1978) *The History of Sexuality: Volume 1: The Will To Knowledge.* Translation by Robert Hurley. New York: Random House.

Foucault, Michel. (1980) *Power/Knowledge.* Brighton: Harvester.

Foucault, Michel. (2003). 'Truth and power', in P. Rabinow and N. Rose (eds) *Essential Works of Foucault 1954–1984.* New York: The New Press, pp. 111–133.

Gill, Ros. (2007) 'Postfeminist media culture: Elements of a sensibility', *European Journal of Cultural Studies*, 10, pp. 147–166.

Goffman, Erving. (1963) *Stigma: Notes on the Management of Spoiled Identity.* Englewood Cliffs, NJ: Prentice Hall.

Goldman, Erving. (2013) 'What should we do about revenge porn sites like Texxxan?' *Forbes.com*, 28 January. Available online at: http://www.forbes.com/sites/ericgoldman/2013/01/28/what-should-we-do-about-revenge-porn-sites-like-texxxan/ (accessed 23 May 2013)

Herring, Susan (1999) 'The rhetorical dynamics of gender harassment on-line', *The Information Society*, 15, pp. 151–167.

Herring, Susan. C. (2002) 'Cyber violence: Recognizing and resisting abuse in online environments', *Asian Women*, 14(Summer), pp. 187–212. Available online at: http://ella.slis.indiana.edu/%7Eherring/violence.html (accessed 28 May 2013).

Hill, Kashmir (2009) 'Revenge porn (or: Another reason not to take nude photos)', *Forbes.com*, 2 June. Available online at: http://www.forbes.com/sites/kashmirhill/2009/06/02/revenge-porn-or-another-reason-not-to-take-nude-photos/2/ (accessed 23 May 2013).

Hirschman, Linda (2006) *Get to Work: A Manifesto for Women of the World.* New York, NY: Viking.

James, Richard (2012) 'Revenge porn: The disturbing but predictable conclusion to sexting', *The Metro*, 20 April. Available online at: http://metro.co.uk/2012/04/20/revenge-porn-the-disturbing-but-predictable-conclusion-to-sexting-3822622/ (accessed 23 May 2013).

Jane, Emma A. (2012) ' "You're a ugly whorish slut" – understanding e-bile', *Feminist Media Studies*, 14(4), pp. 531–546

Lahad, Kinneret (2013) 'The single woman's choice as a zero-sum game'. *Cultural Studies*. Available online at: http://www.tandfonline.com/doi/abs/10.1080/09502386.2013.798341#.UcQ3juu7hhE (accessed 18 May 2013).

Levy, Ariel. (2005) *Female Chauvinist Pigs: Women and the Rise of Raunch Culture.* London: Pocket Books.

Lewis-Hasteley, Helen (2011) ' "You should have your tongue ripped out": The reality of sexist abuse online', *New Statesman*, 3 November. Available online at: http://www.newstatesman.com/blogs/helen-lewis-hasteley/2011/11/comments-rape-abuse-women (accessed 28 May 2013).

McCain, Robert (2013) 'Messed-up people make bad choices in disastrously dysfunctional relationships', *theothermccain.com*, 12 January. Available online at: http://theothermccain.com/2013/01/12/messed-up-people-make-bad-choices-in-disastrously-dysfunctional-relationships/ (accessed 23 May).

McRobbie, Angela (2009) *The Aftermath of Feminism: Gender, Culture and Social Change.* London: Sage.

Mulvey, Laura (1975). 'Visual pleasure and narrative cinema', *Screen*, 16(3), pp. 6–18.

Pink Meth (2013) Available online at: http://pinkmeth.doxing.me/ (accessed 3 April 2013).

Press, Andrea and Livingstone, Sonia (2006) 'Taking audience research into the age of new media: Old problems and new challenges', in Mimi White and James Schwoch (eds) *The Question of Method in Cultural Studies.* Oxford: Blackwell, pp. 175–200.

Probyn, Elspeth (1993) 'Choosing choice: Images of sexuality and "choiceoisie" in popular culture', in Sue Fisher and Kathy Davis (eds) *Negotiating at the Margins: The Gendered Discourses of Power and Resistance.* New Brunswick, NJ: Rutgers University Press, pp. 278–294.

Ringrose, Jessica (2011) 'Are you sexy, flirty, or a slut? Exploring "sexualization" and how teen girls perform/negotiate digital sexual identity on social networking sites', in Rosalind Gill and Christina Scharff (eds) *New Femininities: Postfeminism, Neoliberalism and Subjectivity.* London: Palgrave Macmillan. pp. 99–116.

Rosenthal, Edward C. (2005) *The Era of Choice*. Cambridge, MA: MIT Press.

Thiel-Stern, Shayla (2009) 'Femininity out of control on the internet: A critical analysis of media representations of gender, youth, and MySpace.com in international news discourses', *Girlhood Studies*, 2(1), p. 2039.

Van House, Nancy A (2011) 'Feminist HCI meets Facebook: Performativity and social networking sites', *Interacting with Computers*, 23, pp. 422–429.

Wolf, Naomi (1994). *Fire with Fire: New Female Power and How It Will Change the Twenty-First Century*. London: Vintage.

You Got Posted (2013) Available online at: http://ugotposted.com/ (accessed May 2013).

6
Miranda and *Miranda*: Feminism, Femininity and Performance

Rosie White

Ground-breaking feminist work on women and television comedy in the 1990s addressed its potential for subversive, unruly performance, largely focusing on North American stars such as Lucille Ball and Roseanne Arnold (Mellencamp, 1992; Gray, 1994; Rowe, 1995). This chapter, however, is concerned with how British class identities intersect with the femininity and feminism of a contemporary comedy star and her eponymous sitcom – Miranda Hart and *Miranda* (BBC, 2009–2014).[1] If Hart is an 'unruly woman' (Rowe, 1995) she successfully mobilizes discourses of upper middle class Englishness as a means of mitigating the threat of unruly femininity in television comedy. In British comedy, class is always in play, and *Miranda* has come under public scrutiny for its 'middle class' constituency (Cook, 1982; Lockyer, 2010; Frost, 2011). Shortly after his appointment as controller of BBC1 in 2011 Danny Cohen commented that too many sitcoms were about middle class people:

> Sources say that he feels the Beeb is 'too focused on formats about comfortable, well-off middle-class families whose lives are perhaps more reflective of BBC staff than viewers in other parts of the UK', and that we need more of 'what he describes as "blue-collar" comedies'.
>
> (Leith, 2011)

Miranda and Miranda Hart featured heavily in subsequent debates online and in the broadsheet press about class and television comedy, not least because Hart had just won three British Comedy Awards in January 2011 (see, for example, Boyd and Ferguson, 2011; Fletcher, 2011; Frost, 2011). Several commentators were keen to stress the 'universal' quality of Hart's comedy (Frost, 2011) or that it 'wasn't about class' (Fletcher, 2011), but there is a complex intersection of class and gender at play in Hart's work. Fired by these debates, and her phenomenal success, this essay examines Miranda Hart as a contemporary comedy performer and celebrity, tracing how her television character and celebrity persona negotiate femininity and feminism through a particular class identity.[2]

Hart has moved from minor parts in *Smack the Pony* (Channel 4, 1999–2003) and *Nighty Night* (BBC, 2004–2005), to supporting roles in *Hyperdrive* (BBC, 2006–2007) and *Not Going Out* (BBC, 2006–), and then to writing and starring in her own television series, *Miranda*, following the success of *Miranda Hart's Joke Shop* on BBC Radio 2 (2007–2008). In addition to her award-winning sitcom Hart has appeared on game show panels, chat shows and the BBC's *Comic Relief*, reinforcing a celebrity persona that appears to confirm the identification of the 'real' Miranda Hart with the sitcom character. Beyond television Miranda Hart is a multimedia phenomenon, with a Twitter account (although she professes to despise Twitter), a website, a best-selling autobiography and another volume on the way. She is preparing for a stand-up arena tour in 2014 that is currently selling out, and has stated an ambition to appear in a West End show. She is associate producer on *Miranda* and was executive producer of the documentary *My Hero* (BBC, 2013), which featured Hart talking about her inspiration, comedian Eric Morecambe. In September 2013 Hart hosted a show in BBC1's prime Saturday night slot which celebrated the career of veteran entertainer Bruce Forsyth. *Miranda Meets Bruce* cemented Hart's profile as a mainstream celebrity comedy performer, framing her as a natural successor to an older generation of light entertainment television stars such as Morecambe and Forsyth. Is there nothing Miranda Hart can't do? All of this is the more remarkable considering the historical dominance of male comedy stars in sitcoms and the distinct minority of female comedians on British television panel shows and in stand-up. Hart is already garnering academic attention; there were papers on *Miranda* at *Television for Women*, May 2013, and at *Console-Ing Passions*, June 2013, as well as an essay in a 2012 issue of the journal *Comedy Studies* (Gray, 2012; Becker, 2013; Larrea, 2013; White, 2013).

If she is so far outside the 'norm' of postfeminist celebrity culture, what is it about Miranda that has made it possible for her to become a star in a field dominated by male comics? Hart's strategic deployment of her class persona provides one answer to the enigma of her success. Academic work on stardom and celebrity in film and television notes the negotiation of both extraordinary and ordinary characteristics; that such figures are distant and familiar, unreachable and accessible (Dyer, 1979; Stacey, 1994; Bennett, 2008). The deployment of social media such as Twitter has made this accessibility ever more tantalizingly proximate. Hart has attempted to distance herself from her sitcom character but, even as she does so, she repeatedly endorses her contiguity with Miranda. Miranda Hart has produced a persona that embeds the performance of the sitcom character as part of the 'real' Miranda Hart. She has successfully negotiated a seamless account of the 'television actor or star and the television personality' – playing 'herself' with little apparent distinction between on-screen and private personas (Bennett, 2008, p. 35). Hart's construction of her celebrity persona and sitcom character in terms of upper middle class white Englishness is a large part of their appeal; this essay seeks to map how those classed and raced identities work to mitigate the 'problem' of Hart's gender and offer a 'universal' comedy which reaches a range of audiences.

At first sight Hart's success appears unlikely and remarkable; Hart's celebrity persona, like her character comedy, contradicts the dictates of contemporary media culture that women on screen be small, slight, demure and disciplined. The physical clowning which runs throughout *Miranda* frequently focuses on her body, with scenes of semi-nudity and falling over; every social setting offers an opportunity for embarrassing body-comedy, whether it be farting, nervous laughter or repeated pratfalls. The social milieu in which the series is set evokes an upper middle class environment in which embarrassment is a constant threat but also a marker of authenticity. Miranda's embarrassments, her literal and metaphorical exposures, make her both a comic figure and an 'everywoman', as Hart's performance runs counter to and, at the same time, is reliant upon what Rosalind Gill calls 'postfeminist media culture' and its 'obsessional preoccupation with the body':

> In today's media it is possession of a 'sexy body' that is presented as women's key (if not sole) source of identity. The body is presented simultaneously as women's source of power *and* as always already unruly and requiring constant monitoring, surveillance, discipline and remodelling (and constant spending) in order to conform to ever narrower judgements of female attractiveness.
>
> (2007, p. 255)

Hart's character on screen and her celebrity persona may be read as resistant to and a commentary upon that postfeminist body; her performance as Miranda in the sitcom embodies comic unruliness, constantly falling over, farting, getting tangled up with objects, or exposing her underwear (Rowe, 1995). In her physical comedy Miranda Hart transgresses the alleged 'norm' of the controlled postfeminist body; and as a woman on television who is not short or slim, she visibly contradicts postfeminist imperatives of bodily discipline and self-surveillance. This postfeminist regime is closely aligned with neoliberalism: 'a mobile, calculated technology for governing subjects who are constituted as self-managing, autonomous and enterprising' (Gill and Scharff, 2011, p. 5). The new popular 'postfeminist sensibility' figures femininity as:

> a bodily property; a shift from objectification to subjectification in the ways that (some) women are represented; an emphasis upon self-surveillance, monitoring and discipline; a focus upon individualism, choice and empowerment; the dominance of a 'makeover paradigm'; a resurgence of ideas of natural sexual difference; the marked 'resexualization' of women's bodies; and an emphasis upon consumerism and the commodification of difference. These themes coexist with, and are structured by, stark and continuing inequalities and exclusions that relate to race and ethnicity, class, age, sexuality and disability as well as gender....
>
> (Gill and Scharff, 2011, p. 4)

Hart's comedy offers a critique of that 'sexy body', that shift from 'objectification to subjectification in the ways that (some) women are represented', as *Miranda* directly comments on the television culture that endorses these neoliberal postfeminist regimes, most specifically the 'makeover paradigm'.

The first episode of the first series satirizes lifestyle programming with a parody of *What Not to Wear* (BBC, 2001–2007). This British fashion makeover series, subsequently franchised on American television (TLC, 2003–), was internationally syndicated, featuring the original presenters, Trinny Woodall and Susannah Constantine, in series one to five. Self-help guides based on the show made the Christmas bestseller lists from 2002 to 2004 and Trinny and Susannah appeared regularly on *The Oprah Winfrey Show* (CBS, 1986–2011) after they left *What Not to Wear*. *What Not to Wear* followed a now-standard format for makeover lifestyle programming, first deriding the participants for their poor choices, then teaching them how to shop and dress in a more acceptable manner, followed by a final 'reveal' of their new, improved looks. Martin Roberts notes 'the degree to which contemporary reality and lifestyle television have taken on the role of policing identities and behaviour and their success in reconfiguring these in accordance with the economic interests of neoliberal capitalism' (2007, p. 244; see also Palmer, 2004). The 'makeover paradigm' saturates postfeminist popular culture, presenting narratives of individual transformation as a solution to structural inequalities.

In *Miranda*, Miranda's love interest, Gary, asks her to dinner. Gary says it is not a date but Miranda decides to treat it as such, throwing herself into a frenzy of preparation. In a monologue to camera Miranda says she is going to 'Trinny and Susannah' herself:

> Miranda: 'I couldn't do it with them because I'd have to punch them in the face. Hate those kinds of programmes. [adopts American accent] "Welcome to I'm okay, you're obese." I know what I'd do if I had one of those shows....'
> [cut to Miranda with a microphone and a cameraman, running up to a woman on a busy city street]
> Miranda: 'Excuse me ... Hello. Right, let's have a look at you. Well, I wouldn't wear that top, but you look comfortable – are you?'
> Woman: 'Yeah.'
> Miranda: 'Do *you* like it?'
> Woman: 'Yeah.'

Miranda: 'Do you care that others may not like it?'
Woman: 'No.'
Miranda: 'Brilliant, then, wear that then. Bye. [to cameraman] Right, come on. This is going really well.'

This sequence echoes academic critiques, such as Angela McRobbie's analysis of the 'postfeminist symbolic violence' of shows such as *What Not to Wear* and their 'new hierarchies of taste and style' (2009, p. 127). McRobbie argues that makeover shows mark a shift in the requirements of Western femininity:

> The 'movement of women' refers to the need for women, particularly those who are under the age of 50, and thus still of potential value to the labour market, to come, or move forward, as active participants in these labour markets, and also in consumer culture, since the disposable income permits new realms of buying and shopping. Both of these activities, working and spending, become defining features of new modes of female citizenship.
>
> (2009, p. 124)

McRobbie also notes the class economy of this 'movement of women':

> Working-class women and lower middle-class women, who once tried to achieve simply 'respectability', as Skeggs (1997) argued, as a class-appropriate habitus of femininity, a solution to the tyranny of imposed yet unachievable norms of femininity, which eluded them, are now urged ... to aspire to 'glamorous individuality'.
>
> (2009, p. 125)

The class dynamic of makeover shows is rarely acknowledged within lifestyle programming yet the remit of series about food, decor, gardening and fashion overtly addresses the attempted transformation of lower class taste into something more acceptably bourgeois. Thus the menu is Mediterranean, the colour scheme on-trend, the garden aesthetically pleasing and the fashion 'tasteful' (Skeggs, 2004, p. 141; Roberts, 2007; Powell and Prasad, 2010).

The *Miranda* sequence effectively lampoons the makeover paradigm regarding its gender dynamic, but it elides the class aspect of the format. Miranda presents herself as supportive of the woman in the street's choice of top *even though* she wouldn't wear it herself, thus implying that the top is, indeed, in poor taste. The woman Miranda approaches conforms to the sort of participant often seen on shows such as *What Not to Wear*; she is white, overweight, without apparent make-up and with her hair scraped back in a ponytail, all of which visually codes her as lower class. The woman frowns into the glare of the camera and offers monosyllabic replies. She is emblematic of the 'subjectification' visible in postfeminist makeover shows, and which those shows fail to acknowledge: the class transformations that they rehearse (Palmer, 2004; Powell and Prasad, 2010). While the *Miranda* sketch satirizes the makeover paradigm it reiterates such shows' class discourse, because Miranda is from a similar social background to Trinny and Susannah. Like many presenters on lifestyle television, Miranda is white, educated and upper middle class; her 'unfeminine' size and shape, which is the focus of this episode and of the series, is foregrounded here so that she is represented as an ally of the woman-in-the-street – as an everywoman figure. The caveat in the script, however, is that Miranda would not wear the same top as the woman she confronts with her microphone; while Miranda is more forgiving (and less interventionist) than Trinny and Susannah, she is still positioned as the arbiter of taste, effectively giving the other woman *permission* to be 'comfortable' and 'wear that then'. This short sequence is critical of neoliberal postfeminism, with its insistence on regulation and self-transformation; yet it reiterates a class discourse which is equally problematic. Miranda speaks to, and for, a white Englishness which is predicated on upper middle class 'common sense' as opposed to the consumer capitalism of postfeminist makeovers.

The dynamic of this sequence may also be construed in feminist academic work which pits 'outsider' second wave feminism against the exigencies of consumerist postfeminist desires. There is an odd echo in the *Miranda* sketch of an implicitly classed hierarchy which haunts academic studies:

> Whether postfeminism is seen as anti-feminism or in terms of the contradictory ways in which feminism is manifested in the popular, many studies retain an implicit or explicit assumption that popular culture could still benefit from a 'proper' feminist

makeover. Underpinning many discussions of popular feminism is the assumption that there is a better 'unpopular' form of feminism.... This reproduces the idea that the feminist has good sense and therefore the moral authority to legislate on gendered relations, and also reproduces hierarchical power relations between 'the feminist' situated outside the popular and 'the ordinary woman' located within it.

(Hollows and Moseley, 2006, p. 11)

Joanne Hollows and Rachel Moseley are addressing the relation between popular culture per se and feminist academics' examination of it, but this passage harbours an uncanny reflection on Miranda's feminist 'good sense' in the sequence quoted above. In positioning herself as a 'feminist' character (although not named as such), Hart occupies a dangerous position. The stereotyped 'feminist' is often imagined in popular media as a monstrous other, just as 'proper' feminism asserts its difference from its popular sisters (McRobbie, 2009, pp. 24–53). Hart does not name her comedy as feminist, and proposes it as 'common sense' – however several academics have noted the feminist tendencies of *Miranda* in their commentaries on her work (Gray, 2012; Becker, 2013; Larrea, 2013). The hunger evident in academic and popular responses to *Miranda* undoubtedly demonstrates the paucity of popular alternatives to a mediatized culture awash with airbrushed images of women. Hart's class identity, like that of her character in *Miranda*, enables her to voice a feminist critique of neoliberal postfeminism but is problematic because it speaks *from* and *for* the unacknowledged authority of a specific class position. As Gareth Palmer notes in his critique of lifestyle television: 'This is the power of the norm operated by the middle class, those whose taste determines an increasing number of areas' (2004, p. 184). In these terms the celebration of Hart's feminist politics may be premature, as any challenge to the 'norm' the sitcom character and the celebrity offer is always already reincorporated by the cultural capital of Hart's class identity.

A critique of neoliberal postfeminism is also visible in Hart's autobiography, *Is It Just Me?*, a Christmas 2012 best-seller. The book addresses what Hart calls 'the real coalface of life' (2012, p. 17), with witty analysis of everyday embarrassments and confusions.

The autobiography is now a standard marker of the celebrity comic (see, for example, McPartlin and Donnelly, 2010; Fey, 2011; Kaling, 2011; Walliams, 2013). As Sarah Silverman notes in the preface to her bestselling autobiography, *The Bedwetter*, 'I'm not writing this book to share wisdom or to inspire people. I'm writing this book because I am a famous comedian, which is how it works now' (2010, p. xiv). Hart's autobiographical narrative closely mirrors the verbal style of *Miranda*, which also topped Christmas 2012 ratings, beating off *Downton Abbey*, *Dr Who* and *Strictly Come Dancing*. Several chapters of *Is It Just Me?* address feminist concerns about the beauty industry, body image and the social construction of femininity, with titles such as 'Beauty', 'Bodies', 'Exercise' and 'Diet'. The book as a whole argues against a consumerist femininity which is thin, passive and neurotic. In Chapter 6, 'Beauty', Hart addresses the concept of 'taking myself seriously as a woman', asking what that phrase entails:

> Is it a fine lady scientist, a ballsy young anarchist with tights on her head or a feminist intellectual from the 1970s nose-down in Simone de Beauvoir? Or is it what I think my friend meant when she said 'woman', which is really 'aesthetic object'. Clothes horse. Show pony. General beautiful piece of well-groomed stuff that's lovely to look at?
>
> (2012, pp. 94–95)

What follows is a comic deconstruction of the rigours of feminine grooming, examining spas, hairdressing salons and the beauty myth, pointing out the gender imbalance at work here:

> And – I must ask – do *men* have to do this? Is this a thing for them, too? What would it mean to 'take yourself seriously as a man'? Let's see. Attention All Men – please put down the *Top Gear* annual and join me in a round of 'Say It Out Loud With Miranda'. Lean back, and growl 'I am taking myself seriously as a man.' What springs to mind? Is it a singlet, a tool belt and a roll of electrical tape? Or is it a sharp suit, a cocktail, and the presidency of the International Monetary Fund? Or perhaps you suddenly feel the need to hole up in a dingy pub and start yelling 'Ref!' at the telly? Whatever it is, it's not likely to have much to do with grooming,

or carrying a particular type of slightly-too-small and essentially useless bag masquerading as a clutch (good word).

(2012, p. 95)

Hart proposes a manifesto in which clothing is governmental standard issue (one outfit for weekdays, another for weekends, and a unisex party kaftan), and anti-ageing treatments involve eating roast dinners, doughnuts and buttered toast on the principle that 'Fat Don't Crack' (2012, pp. 115–116). *Is It Just Me?* states that there are advantages for women of not being considered 'beautiful' in contemporary consumer culture. During an ongoing dialogue with her younger self Hart states: 'IT IS FAR, FAR BETTER NEVER TO HAVE BEEN BEAUTIFUL' (2012, p. 100). Even as she acknowledges that 'a professional sociologist [would] fling their pencil aside in despair' at the oversimplification of this assertion, Hart proposes that it confers an invisibility which offers women time and space in which to do something a bit more constructive than address the rigours of postfeminist self-scrutiny and grooming:

> space that you can constructively use to discover and hone your skills, learn a language, develop an interest in cosmology, practise the oboe, do whatever you fancy, really, so long as it doesn't involve being looked at or snogging anyone. And you'll very likely emerge from your chrysalis aged twenty-five as a highly accomplished young thing ready to take on the world. Meanwhile, The Beautiful Ones will have been so busy having boyfriends and brushing their hair that they'll just be…who they always were.
>
> (2012, pp. 100–101)

In this comic scenario, the makeover paradigm is transformed from the consumerist ethic of shows like *What Not to Wear* to an upper middle class Protestant work ethic where culture and education, rather than shopping, is transformative.

Miranda's feminist makeover of postfeminist regimes of appearance is thus negotiated though a class discourse which is reclaimed even as it is disavowed. Languages, cosmology and the oboe seem unlikely options for a working class teenager, but, as in the sitcom, the 18 year-old Miranda in *Is It Just Me?* is framed within a cartoonishly drawn upper middle class environment. She introduces herself as: 'Six feet tall, thin as a rail, school-issue straw boater, one red, one green sock, and a lacrosse stick slung over my shoulder', and is greeted by the older Miranda: 'How absolutely lovely to see you in all your *Mallory Towers* [*sic*] finery' (2012, p. 6). The reference to Enid Blyton's *Malory Towers* series set in a girls' boarding school is significant as it situates Miranda as stereotypically upper middle class, calling upon nostalgic images of 1940s and 1950s childhood, while simultaneously lampooning that tradition. Much like the 'ironic dismissal' performed by male sitcom characters to acknowledge homoerotic behaviour even as they deny its implications, this technique manages Miranda's class identity by simultaneously acknowledging it and refuting it as a category (Miller, 2006). British television's comic deployment of class stereotypes has a long history; most notably, the 'alternative' comedians of the 1980s launched a critique of middle class narratives through satirizing Enid Blyton in television programmes such as *The Comic Strip Presents: Five Go Mad in Dorset* (Channel 4, 1982). This first episode in a series of self-contained comedy dramas, all prefaced with *The Comic Strip Presents...*, featured comedians from London's Comic Strip Club, most of whom went on to become household names, including Adrian Edmondson, Dawn French, Jennifer Saunders and Peter Richardson. While the series relied on its audience's knowledge of and nostalgia for Enid Blyton's *Famous Five* books, it also parodied the reactionary politics of Blyton's characters, who were always suspicious of foreigners and the lower class. In *Five Go Mad in Dorset*, the misogyny, homophobia, racism and snobbery of the originals are made manifest; *Five Go Mad on Mescalin* was screened the following year, and the series helped to cement Channel 4's early reputation as a youth-oriented, taboo-breaking broadcaster. In *Miranda* and *Is It Just Me*, however, Hart's upper middle class background is deployed somewhat differently, to signify a nostalgic return to 'common sense'; it is removed from its political history and employed to confer authority and authenticity on Miranda as narrator.

The focus on Miranda as authentic moral voice is evident in the visual style of the sitcom; the to-camera narrative style of *Miranda* has been widely noted (Becker, 2013), as has Miranda's authoritative position as narrator:

> She breezily starts each episode by welcoming the viewer, going through the motions of politely asking after us but brusquely

adding that she's not really interested, before taking control of her visibility by launching the opening credits and declaring, 'On with the show'. Everything we see is with her consent; frequent looks to camera remind us of this; she uses cameras like punctuation marks to fine-tune the comic structure to her satisfaction.

(Gray, 2012, p. 195)

Hart's ability to construct a character so apparently at ease with and in command of the television camera is irrevocably linked to her class identity. From the outset, Hart's background has repeatedly been addressed in articles and interviews. In an early interview for *The Lady* Hart asserts that 'the British middle class is a great source of humour' while her interviewer adds that 'It is precisely because she embraces her middle-class privileged background that the show stands out' (Jonzen, 2009, p. 25). More recently the *Daily Express* ran a story about the 'Tragedy and despair behind Miranda Hart's rise to the top':

Behind Miranda Hart's steady rise to the top lies a genuine tale of overcoming the odds, with the star beating depression and dealing with the horror of nearly losing her father in the Falklands War. . . . She says she is from an upper-class background, but does not consider herself upper-class. Her mother, Diana, is the daughter of Sir William Luce, a former governor of Aden.

(Roche, 2012)

Hart has repeatedly 'come out' as middle class; here her class identity – she went to the same private school as Claire Balding and her father was a senior officer in the Royal Navy – is commuted with reference to her 'journey' through depression and family trauma. In *The Lady* she also discussed her depression and agoraphobia. Class is thus always visible in *Miranda* and in Hart's press interviews, but framed in a manner which asserts the authority of middle class identity even as it is mitigated by a range of strategies. In *The Lady*, for example, with its constituency of middle class readers (or readers who aspire to a particular fantasy middle class lifestyle), Miranda is commended for her honesty in embracing 'her middle-class privileged background'. In an interview profile for liberal broadsheet *The Independent*, Hart again acknowledges her class background but also asserts her 'classlessness':

I suppose my thing is to make sure it's as universal as possible. I only really think comedy's got a problem if the central character is middle-class and her values are only middle-class and then people aren't going to relate or be interested. This character is completely classless really. She happens to be from Surrey but her goals and her fears and her problems could happen to anybody.

(Gilbert, 2011)

This 'classless' identity is reiterated in the *Daily Mirror* where Hart is cited as saying that she's 'from an upper-class background, but does not consider herself upper-class', although this is placed somewhat ironically before the description of her as the granddaughter of 'Sir William Luce, a former governor of Aden' (Roche, 2012). All the extended profiles of Hart make mention of her struggle with depression and anxiety, and her father's war experience in the Falklands, creating a narrative of Hart's 'journey' to success – a narrative not unlike that of the makeover paradigm, but framed in very different terms.

Beverley Skeggs, in her work on class and culture, argues that in a popular landscape heavily weighted against the working class – usually represented as excessive, wasteful, fecund, unable to change, tasteless and (perhaps for all these reasons) authentic – the middle class has one particular pejorative characteristic to negotiate: pretentiousness. Nineteenth-century music hall comedy acts critiqued 'the uptight restrained middle-class', helping to establish a tradition which addressed pretension and snobbery as a source of humour (Skeggs, 2004, p. 114). Following the 'alternative' comedy of the 1980s, where class and politics were again to the fore, British middle class television comedians have negotiated their class identity in particular ways:

So Adam Buxton and Joe Cornish (of the cult *Adam and Joe Show*) when interviewed in the *Guardian* (15 September 2001, p. 11), reflect on their fan base and argue that they were categorized (unfairly, they thought) as 'unfashionably middle class and too posh...It's just because we are this sort of nebulous item, so people fixate on the school we went to and think "Oh they're not northern, they're not stand-up, they're not anything really, so let's make them slacker toffs".' To make sure that the reader and interviewer understand their ironic take on such matters they add: 'Fair enough really.'

(Skeggs, 2004, pp. 114–115)

This ironic acknowledgement of middle class identity is necessary in a cultural milieu where to be middle class and 'cool' is an oxymoron (Skeggs, 2004, p. 115). Yet *Miranda* trades on not being 'cool'; as Gerald Gilbert states in the interview for *The Independent*:

> While the critics traded endless permutations on the words 'slapstick', 'old-fashioned' and 'acquired taste', Miranda built up a devoted word-of-mouth audience able to appreciate her humour without tying themselves up in knots to justify their enjoyment of something seemingly so old-school and uncool.
>
> (Gilbert, 2011)

These categories – 'old-school and uncool' – help to delineate the particular strategies at play in the packaging of Hart's celebrity persona and her sitcom's popularity. Far from refuting her class identity, Hart deploys it to inform the narrative language and style of *Miranda*. Despite her many assertions that her character is 'classless' or that comedy is not about class, her success is reliant on responses to British upper middle identity as authoritative, eccentric and endearing (see, for example, Fletcher, 2011). Hart's comedy, like her femininity, is thus understood through its iteration of white upper middle class Englishness. Her family background inextricably anchors her to the history of Empire and secures Hart more firmly within the class identity that her role as Camilla 'Chummy' Fortescue-Cholmondley-Browne in *Call the Midwife* (BBC, 2012–) serves to confirm; a 'retro' white middle class persona which entails the aesthetic of a fictional public school. This is an imaginary England where people speak in RP, quaff (not drink) ginger beer, and believe in fair play. It calls upon a nostalgia that is most evident in Hart's playful use of language, harking back to a fictional upper middle class pre-feminist era which, while framed in terms of an 'ironic dismissal' is nevertheless invoked. The repeated 'Such fun!' uttered by Miranda's mother (Patricia Hodge) has become one of the show's catchphrases. This aspect of *Miranda* fits with neo-traditional femininities evident in other television formats, such as cookery and makeover shows (see Brunsdon, 2006; Hollows, 2006; Smith, 2011). Neo-traditional references are also apparent in the comparisons made by Hart and others about the style of comedy she evokes; most frequently Morecambe and Wise, but also Joyce Grenfell and Hattie Jacques. Hart is rarely compared to more contemporary comedians, although Jennifer Saunders was allegedly instrumental in helping her break through with her Radio 2 series, which led to the television sitcom (Jonzen, 2009).

This makes for an odd juxtaposition with the 'feminist' discourse evident in Hart's sitcom and autobiography. Or maybe not. It is that classed voice which makes Miranda and *Miranda* intelligible within the terms of postfeminist media culture. Her class identity makes a feminist discourse speakable and legible in popular culture via the popular romance of English heritage television; not just *Call the Midwife* but the nostalgic appeal of shows such as *Downton Abbey* (ITV, 2010–) and *Upstairs Downstairs* (LWT, 1971–1975; BBC, 2010–2012). In its own way *Miranda* is also an historical drama, situated in a fantasy of Englishness underpinned by Hart's upper class eccentricity. The cultural capital of Hart's class identity enables her to *speak* feminist; it situates that speech in a political vacuum where gender issues can be raised without consequences. In *Gender and the Media* Rosalind Gill notes how 'feminism is now part of the cultural field' but also how it has become 'incorporated, revised and depoliticised' (2007, p. 268). Hart's celebrity persona, like her sitcom, speaks to a 1950s 'common sense' which repudiates the demands of postfeminist media culture – to be groomed, self-regulating and under control – while conveniently forgetting the historical realities of the fifties, or the political work of second wave feminism. Lynn Spigel remarks on a similar dynamic at work in more explicitly nostalgic television series, such as *Mad Men* (AMC, 2007–), where the narrative offers a postfeminist nostalgia for a pre-feminist past without acknowledging the existence of feminist struggles in between:

> Contemporary nostalgia offers a strange form of time travel. Moving back to a fantasy future imagined sometime in the baby-boom past, it is easy to lose track of where you are. The most unfortunate consequence of this new form of nostalgia is that despite its sophisticated cosmopolitanism and aspiring 'liberated' career girls, it forgets feminism as a political struggle – both its battles

against patriarchal injustices and its own internal struggles among women of different sexual orientations and from different class, racial, national, religious and political backgrounds. Prefeminism and postfeminism without the feminism in the middle is a hard thing to imagine. But somehow, much of contemporary nostalgia culture seems to be just that.

(2013, p. 278)

Hart's work does not offer the glossy surfaces of a series like *Mad Men* but her narrative calls upon nostalgia for a pre-feminist television culture as a means of railing against postfeminist excesses. The commentaries which *Miranda* and Hart's autobiography offer on the demands made of women and girls (and sometimes of men and boys) to conform to a bizarre celebrity version of 'normal' are framed within a pre-feminist sensibility. Most notably, her work avoids directly addressing issues of race and class.

This negotiation of pre-feminist, feminist and postfeminist television femininities is executed through a complex deployment of comedy tropes and references, not least of which is the confessional telling of the self. In the to-camera narration, and in the chummy first-person narrative of *Is It Just Me?*, *Miranda* and Miranda Hart deploy the tradition of confession as a means of constituting the self. As Skeggs argues, this is a classed process, available to those with access to middle class resources (2004, pp. 120–127): 'self-narration was also strongly related to the construction of "character" and "personhood", whereby only the bourgeoisie were seen to be capable of being individuals' (Skeggs, 2004, p. 124). Miranda the sitcom character and Miranda Hart the celebrity are presented via self-consciously playful textual performances, playing with language and foregrounding particular words or phrases. Skeggs examines textual strategies within contemporary feminist research; approaches which reflexively 'de-centre the singular voice of the researcher by using a variety of literary techniques of dialogism', arguing that this is another means of demonstrating cultural authority:

Textual demonstration displays the cleverness of the writer, whilst also supposedly de-centering the author at the same time. This is not just a matter of the powerful claiming marginality. Rather it is about the powerful showing how well they understand power by playing with it. It is a matter of having your authority and eating it.

(Skeggs, 2004, p. 131)

The power of narrating the self in these de-centred times is manifold: by doing so one can reposition oneself as an emblematic figure while ostensibly disclaiming the privilege that made such a manoeuvre possible.

This would seem to produce a damning critique of Miranda Hart's success – that is not my intention. Rather I want to propose this as an explanation *for* her extraordinary success, not just with *Miranda* but also across the field of popular celebrity. Hart's alignment with Bruce Forsyth places her at the pinnacle of the BBC's current television stars, and may indicate the corporation's perception of her as a possible panacea to be deployed against the negative press they have received following recent scandals about mismanagement, institutional sexism and paedophilia. Skeggs argues that the reflexive narration of self in contemporary culture:

> offers a re-traditionalization of gender, class and sexual relations.... The logic of this experimental individualism (or the prosthetic self) for those who can tool themselves up is that disembedding, de-racination, de-gendering and de-classing is possible, even at a time when such classifications are becoming more acute for those at the extreme ends of the social scale.

(2004, p. 133)

In these terms *Miranda* and Miranda Hart represent a timely configuration of comedy and celebrity, offering audiences a seemingly de-raced, de-gendered and de-classed entertainment in a period of widespread austerity. The *Daily Express* profile notes Hart's mass appeal, quoting 'Jack O'Toole, a 19-year-old student from Newcastle', who claims that she is 'must-see viewing on campus': ' "She just seems one of the most humble and genuine celebrities out there," he added. "And very funny to people of all ages" ' (Roche, 2012). Once again, this reiterated endorsement of Hart's humility and authenticity – her lack of middle class pretentiousness – and her 'universal' appeal, positions her as outside social categories; as, simply, a star who transcends the everyday. This configuration elides the labour of *making* television; Miranda's 'authenticity' in *Miranda,* as in much of Hart's television work, is carefully crafted and scripted – a 'natural' self which is laboriously constructed. In the same article Hart claims, yet again, that: 'Playing Miranda in *Miranda* – I'm sure some people might not see it as acting but, I assure you, I am.... I very much see it as playing a character.' This protestation offers a feeble resistance to the success of Miranda and *Miranda,* as Hart's celebrity persona is fully aligned with her sitcom character. It is hardly surprising that viewers are convinced that this is an authentic representation of Miranda Hart.

As I write, in November 2013, Hart is preparing for a first stand-up tour (which is already sold out at many venues) in 2014, and has launched an exercise DVD, *Miranda Hart's Maracattack,* featuring new material and guest appearances from her co-stars on *Miranda*: 'Take a firm grip of your maracas and laugh along with comedy queen Miranda Hart' (advertisement in *Metro,* 20 November 2013). Hart has also guest-edited the November 2013 issue of *Stylist,* a free weekly magazine aimed at 'affluent career women' (Magee, 2009). Hart's issue calls on an array of celebrity 'friends' to oversee different sections in a 'celebrity takeover':

> Among other very special treats for you, I have the beyond fab-
> ulous Claudia Winkleman on travel. She was sent to write about
> Rio – tough gig. The lovely Lauren Laverne on food. And she baked
> a cake. With three tiers. Oh yes. Three cheers for her three tiers
> (word play – you're welcome). And in a, what I call *twist,* Nigella
> is Beauty Director. Oh yeah, look at me thinking outside of the
> magazinery box. I hope you enjoy this special edition as much as
> we all enjoyed creating it. I have loved being Editor in Chief of
> Magazinery. I spent the week wearing trouser suits with padded
> shoulder jackets (child of the Eighties), barking orders at an imag-
> inary assistant while clutching a skinny Frappuccino (which I
> always think sounds like a tiny Italian man), and finding the sex-
> iest pose I could at my elegant desk (I only fell off four times).
> It was very much like Meryl Streep in *The Devil Wears Prada.*
>
> (Hart, 2013)

This editorial address is framed in characteristic *Miranda* style, proposing a persona that is still falling off desks and playing with words. In the light of Hart's growing multimedia success, however, her celebrity persona may wear a bit thin, stretched as it is between performance as 'Miranda' and a highly successful (and increasingly svelte) Hart. Miranda Hart's unruly comedy has become a commodity within postfeminist media culture, selling merchandise and fronting a glossy fashion magazine; a shift which denotes the limits of Hart's address to feminist 'common sense' in her sitcom and autobiography. The remarkable success of Miranda and *Miranda* demonstrates how a particular version of bourgeois feminism has been rehabilitated in contemporary popular culture. As Ros Gill observes, 'feminism is now part of the cultural field' but it has become 'incorporated, revised and depoliticised' (2007, p. 268). It would appear that *Miranda* and Miranda articulate precisely the sort of feminism that neoliberal consumer culture can sell.

Notes

1. An earlier version of this paper was presented at *Console-Ing Passions 2013*, 23–25 June, De Montfort University, Leicester, UK.
2. In order to distinguish between the comedy character and the actor I will employ Miranda to refer to the former and Hart to refer to the latter.

Bibliography

Becker, Christine (2013) 'Form, function and cultural legitimation in *Miranda*', Conference Paper Delivered at *Console-Ing Passions 2013*, 23–25 June, De Montfort University, Leicester, UK.

Bennett, James (2008) 'The television personality system: Televisual stardom revisited after film theory', *Screen*, 49(1) (Spring 2008), pp. 32–50.

Brunsdon, Charlotte (2006) 'The feminist in the kitchen: Martha, Martha and Nigella', in Joanne Hollows and Rachel Moseley (eds) *Feminism in Popular Culture*. Oxford and New York: Berg, pp. 41–56.

Cook, Jim (ed.) (1982) *BFI Dossier 17: Television Sitcom*. London: British Film Institute.

Cumming, Edd. (2011) 'Miranda Hart is as funny as a potato – but her popularity proves Britain is still obsessed with class', *The Telegraph*, 24 January 2011. Available online at: http://blogs.telegraph.co.uk/culture/edcummingliterature/100050880/miranda-hart-is-as-funny-as-a-potato-but-her-popularity-proves-britain-is-still-obsessed-with-class/ (accessed 25 September 2013).

Dyer, Richard (1979) *Stars*. London: British Film Institute.

Fey, Tina (2011) *Bossypants*. London: Sphere.

Fletcher, Alex (2011) 'Miranda Hart: "*Miranda* is universal, not middle class"',
Digital Spy, 27 August 2011. Available online at: http://www.digitalspy.co
.uk/tv/news/a337438/miranda-hart-miranda-is-universal-not-middle-class
.html#no (accessed 25 September 2013).

Frost, Vicky (2011) 'TV comedy: Is it really a class issue?', *The Guardian*,
24 January 2011. Available online at: http://www.theguardian.com/tv-and
-radio/tvandradioblog/2011/jan/24/tv-comedy-class-miranda-hart
(accessed 25 September 2013).

Gammell, Caroline (2011) 'BBC to introduce more working class comedy', *The
Telegraph*, 23 January 2011. Available online at: http://www.telegraph.co
.uk/news/uknews/8277022/BBC-to-introduce-more-working-class-comedy
.html (accessed 24 September 2013).

Gilbert, Gerald (2011) 'Miranda Hart: "I was never in the cool gang"',
The Independent, 3 December 2011. Available online at: http://www
.independent.co.uk/news/people/profiles/miranda-hart-i-was-never-in-the
-cool-gang-6270552.html (accessed 25 September 2013).

Gill, Rosalind (2007) *Gender and the Media*. Cambridge: Polity Press.

Gill, Rosalind and Christina Scharff (eds) (2011) *New Femininities:
Postfeminism, Neoliberalism and Subjectivity*. London: Palgrave Macmillan.

Gray, Frances (1994) *Women and Laughter*. Charlottesville: University Press of
Virginia.

Gray, Frances (2012) 'Cameras, reality and *Miranda*', *Comedy Studies*, 3(2),
pp. 191–199.

Hart, Miranda (2012) *Is It Just Me?* London: Hodder and Stoughton.

Hart, Miranda (2013) 'Miranda's editor's letter', *Stylist*, 26 November 2013.
Available online at: http://www.stylist.co.uk/people/miranda-harts-editors
-letter#image-rotator-1 (accessed 30 November 2013).

Hilton, Boyd and Euan Ferguson (2011) 'Are TV sitcoms too middle
class?', *The Observer*, 30 January 2011. Available online at: http://www
.theguardian.com/commentisfree/2011/jan/30/danny-cohen-middle-class
-comedy (accessed 19 November 2013).

Hollows, Joanne (2006)'Can I go home yet? Feminism, post-feminism and
domesticity', in Joanne Hollows and Rachel Moseley (eds) *Feminism in
Popular Culture*. Oxford and New York: Berg, pp. 97–118.

Hollows, Boyd and Rachel Moseley (2006) 'Popularity contests: The meanings
of popular feminism', in Joanne Hollows and Rachel Moseley (eds) *Feminism
in Popular Culture*. Oxford and New York: Berg, pp. 1–22.

Jonzen, Jessica (2009) 'Tall stories', *The Lady*, 8 December 2009, pp. 24–25.

Kaling, Mindy (2011) *Is Everyone Hanging Out Without Me? (And Other Concerns)*. New York: Three Rivers Press.

Larrea, Carlota (2013) '"Big and silly and not afraid of falling over": Genre
and gendered identity in Miranda', Conference Paper Delivered at *Television for Women: An International Conference*, 15–17 May 2013, University of
Warwick.

Leith, Sam (2011) 'Whatever happened to the working class sitcom?',
The Guardian, 24 January 2011. Available online at: http://www.the

guardian.com/tv-and-radio/2011/jan/24/working-class-sitcoms (accessed 19 November 2013).

Lockyer, Sharon (2010) 'Chavs and Chav-nots: Social class in *Little Britain*', in Sharon Lockyer (ed.) *Reading Little Britain*. London: I. B. Tauris, pp. 95–110

Magee, Kate (2009) 'Stylist magazine storms onto free title scene', *PR Week*, 21 October 2009. Available online at: http://www.prweek.com/article/947171/stylist-magazine-storms-free-title-scene (accessed 9 February 2014).

McPartlin, Ant and Declan Donnelly (2010) *Ooh, What a Lovely Pair! Our Story*. London: Penguin.

McRobbie, Angela (2009) *The Aftermath of Feminism: Gender, Culture and Social Change*. London: Sage.

Mellencamp, Patricia (1992) *High Anxiety: Catastrophe, Scandal, Age and Comedy*. Bloomington and Indianapolis: Indiana University Press.

Miller, Margo (2006) 'Masculinity and male intimacy in nineties sitcoms: *Seinfeld* and the ironic dismissal', in James R Kellner and Leslie Stratyner (eds) *The New Queer Aesthetic on Television: Essays on Recent Programming*. Jefferson: McFarland and Company, pp. 147–159.

Palmer, Gareth (2004) ' "The New You": Class and transformation in lifestyle television', in Su Holmes and Deborah Jermyn (eds) *Understanding Reality Television*. London and New York: Routledge, pp. 173–190.

Powell, Helen and Sylvie Prasad (2010) ' "As Seen on TV" the celebrity expert: How taste is shaped by lifestyle media', *Cultural Politics*, 6(1), pp. 111–124.

Roberts, Martin (2007) 'The fashion police: Governing the self in *What Not to Wear*', in Yvonne Tasker and Diane Negra (eds) *Interrogating Postfeminism*. Durham and London: Duke University Press. pp. 227–248.

Roche, Elisa (2012) 'Tragedy and despair behind Miranda Hart's rise to the top', *Daily Express*, 16 February 2012. Available online at: http://www.express.co.uk/news/showbiz/302418/Tragedy-and-despair-behind-Miranda-Hart-s-rise-to-the-top (accessed 24 September 2013).

Rowe, Kathleen (1995) *The Unruly Woman: Gender and the Genres of Laughter*. Austin: University of Texas Press.

Silverman, Sarah (2010) *The Bedwetter: Stories of Courage, Redemption, and Pee*. London: Faber and Faber.

Skeggs, Beverley (2004) *Class, Self, Culture*. London: Routledge.

Smith, Angela (2011) 'Femininity repackaged: Postfeminism and *ladette to lady*', in Melanie Waters (ed.) *Women on Screen: Feminism and Femininity in Visual Culture*. Basingstoke: Palgrave Macmillan, pp. 153–166.

Spigel, Lynn (2013) 'Postfeminist nostalgia for a prefeminist future', *Screen*, 54(2), pp. 270–278.

Stacey, Jackie (1994) *Star Gazing: Hollywood Cinema and Female Spectatorship*. London and New York: Routledge.

Walliams, David (2013) *Camp David*. London: Penguin.

White, Rosie (2013) 'Miranda and *Miranda*: Comedy, femininity and performance', Conference Paper Delivered at *Console-Ing Passions 2013*, 23–25 June, Leicester, UK: De Montfort University.

7
Flexible Femininities? Queering *Kawaii* in Japanese Girls' Culture

Makiko Iseri

While Japanese subculture – especially what is called '*kawaii* (cute) culture' – currently receives global attention, it has been studied most frequently in the context of Japanese *anime/manga* or its appropriation by Japanese contemporary artists (Ngai, 2005), and very few readings of *kawaii* highlight another 'root' of this phenomenon: Japanese girls' culture. This paper will investigate the complicated relationship between the particular modes of feminine gender performance in Japanese girls' culture and its politics of bodily flexibility. What this paper aims, however, is *not* to define what the concept of *kawaii* is; rather, this paper intends to shed light on the way in which the media images of *kawaii* have been visualized as 'the flexible' in today's socioeconomic context, and to explore what is at stake when such 'non-normative' or 'unusual' femininity comes to gain the desirable status of 'flexible body'.

On the one hand, queer studies and anti-foundationalist feminism have called much attention to bodily flexibility as the potential to subvert heterosexist norms, but on the other, the concept of flexibility also signifies the capacity to manage risks and handle a changing situation properly, and its high affinity with neoliberalism is pointed out (Martin, 1994; Halberstam, 2005; McRuer, 2006). Through focusing on the problematic relationship between flexibility and visibility, I will provide a critical analysis of the representation of Japanese *kawaii* culture which is made possible within the complicated power structures of neoliberalism, Orientalism and nationalism.

Bodily politics of femininity, visibility and flexibility

In one respect, the critique of stable and coherent identities is one of the vital foundations of queer theory, while fluid sexuality and flexible gender performance are often celebrated for their potential to subvert conventional norms. In particular, it is notable that there has been much attention paid to cross-gender figures, such as the drag queen, who 'reveal the imitative structure of gender itself – as well as its contingency' (Butler, 1990. p. 187). Here, the historically stigmatized gender performance of the drag queen comes into the limelight as a queer parody, making visible the subversive potential of flexible identity and opening up new possibilities for transforming conventional norms.

While there is no doubt that Butler's theory of gender performativity suggests the alternative way of thinking about our body, identity and desire, its tendency to privilege the cross-gender figure as a visible signifier of radical queerness has been criticized from various points of view. Biddy Martin (1996), for example, draws our attention to a question that is difficult to avoid: at what cost can queer sexuality, as represented by gender crossing, become flexible, transgressive and thus subversive? In the atmosphere of privileging visible difference as radical queerness, she warns, 'the feminine' or 'the female body' is assumed to be a 'fixed ground' (Martin, 1996, p. 72); the queerness of femme lesbians is often made invisible because their gender performance seems like 'comfort with the female body' (Martin, 1996, p. 90) and thus lacks visual 'evidence' of subversiveness. Martin's argument reveals the tendency of queer studies to privilege the visible difference from conventional norms and how such dependence on visibility results, despite its political intention, in a failure to theorize the queerness of femininity.

When we look at recent pop culture in Japan, however, feminine gender performance acted out by the female body now seems to start gaining a certain kind of visibility and to be represented as 'the flexible'. This might look, at first glance, quite similar to the phenomenon called postfeminism, in which girls' culture and female femininity have been re-appraised as hyperfemininity. Although it is easy to position Japanese *kawaii* culture in the genealogy of postfeminism, as some critics actually do (Brown, 2011), it can be misleading to understand their femininity simply as hyperfemininity. This is not just because of its dependence on the specific (largely Euro-American) context, but also because the styles of *kawaii* generated in Japanese girls' culture have all too often been regarded as obviously deviant from – or resistant against – ideal femininity in Japanese society, and hence they should be distinguished from the '[p]ost-feminist, neo-liberal notions of femininity [which] often demand that girls are hyperfeminine, that is, heterosexually desirable' (Holland and Harpin, 2013, p. 7), like female characters in *Sex and the City* or the Spice Girls.

I would like to note quickly, however, it is not my intention to articulate femininity in Japanese *kawaii* culture as more radically non-normative and thus subversive compared to hyperfemininity in Euro-American postfeminist culture, which is criticized for being 'too similar' to patriarchal ideals of feminine beauty (Genz and Brabon, 2009, p. 79). The terminology of hyperfemininity is often defined as 'exaggerated adherence to a stereotypical feminine gen-der role' (Murnen and Byrne, 1991, p. 479) or 'a marker of the worst excesses of hegemonic femininity' (Holland and Harpin, 2013, p. 1). Here, it is obvious that the subversive potential of hyperfemininity lies in its distance from normative femininity, which is maintained by (visual/visible) exaggeration or excess of the latter. However, as Carole-Anne Tyler comments, it is precisely 'a parodic or ironic exaggeration or hyperbolization of gender' which is often achieved by distributing ' "unnaturally bad" taste' (='excess') to 'working-class women or women of color', and that paradoxically serves to 'reinscribe white, middle-class femininity as a real thing, the (quint)essence of femininity' (2003, p. 105).

Therefore, what we need to interrogate is, instead of differentiating liberated hyperfemininity from a 'trapped' feminine gender role, the problematic way in which *kawaii* femininity is celebrated is precisely by its visible difference (or distance) from what counts as natural femininity, exploiting 'other' bodies to the neoliberal and nation-alistic discourses. Flexible femininity in Japanese *kawaii* culture is neither a sign of liberation nor progress, but rather constitutes the very site/sight where bodily flexibility is achieved within complicated power structures of Orientalism, nationalism and neoliberalism. Through tracing the genealogy of Japanese girls' culture in the media, I shall provide a critical analysis of the contradictory images of *kawaii*, which is regarded as both a consuming *and* consumable figure of 'otherness', being indivisibly united with female bodies and particular images of Japanese-ness.

Genealogy of Japanese girls' culture and reinventing the *kawaii*

Contemporary Japanese girls' culture and its particular modes of femininity, created and developed since the mid-1990s, as this paper will emphasize, can be understood as a youth resistance culture, especially against the dominant norms of ideal or traditional femininity required of women in Japanese society. Its particular fashion mode and lifestyle among the young girls seem to reflect interests shared with feminism in many respects, and their self-expression through visibly non-normative gender performances has received both criticism and appreciation. Because of the recent trend to celebrate Japanese girls' culture as creative, unique and flexible, accompanied by both global and domestic commercialization of the participants, resistance through the cultural practice of female-female impersonation is now in danger of being normalized into neoliberal and nationalistic discourses. Before moving on to an analysis of such (re-)reappropriation of the girls' culture by neoliberal capitalism and national politics in Japan, I shall provide a brief summary of some characteristics of Japanese girls' culture from the mid-1990s to the 2000s, and trace the way they have been regarded in Japanese society.

Gyaru culture: Deviant femininities as a strategy for survival

One of the roots of Japanese girls' culture can be found in the *gyaru* (gal) culture generated from the streets of Shibuya, one of the trendy youth districts in Tokyo. It became very popular among teenage girls across Japan especially from the late 1990s to the early 2000s. Their fashion styles are usually characterized as follows:

> First of all, over 4 inch-tall platform sandals or boots. Bright coloured, skimpy outfits such as a micro-mini skirt. Extremely bleached blond or white hair. Glittering makeup. Furthermore, their faces are incredibly dark for Japanese – that is not made by makeup but artificial tanning.
>
> (AERA, 1999, p. 35)

The girls dressed up in this fashion are called '*ganguro*' or '*gonguro*' *gyaru*, which means literally 'black face', and the Japanese media repeatedly reported their deviant fashion and lifestyle, commenting on them as corrupt, immature, dirty and delinquent crazy women who were destroying the morals of Japanese society.[1]

From the early 2000s, some of these girls moved into a new style. The emergence of the girls called *yamanba*, which literally means 'mountain hag', a man-eating witch in Japanese folklore, is known as the most extreme form of *gyaru* culture. *Yamanba* fashion style shocked Japanese society: the girls were panda-eyed, with 'fluorescent and white makeup around their eyes, on their lips, and in a strip down their nose' (Keet, 2007, p. 10) in vivid contrast to their heavily tanned dark skin, coloured contact lenses and the shiny stickers decorating their faces (Macias and Evers, 2007, p. 83). On the one hand, such a peculiar mode of self-expression by the *gonguro* and *yamanba* received enthusiastic support by teenage girls through the spread of the fashion magazine *egg* (1995–), which has had a very powerful influence on the *gyaru* generation, becoming the 'bible' for *gyaru* girls; at the same time, *gyaru* culture with its non-normative gender performance was also targeted for misogynistic hostility and derision by the mainstream media.[2]

It is precisely because of such deviant gender expressions, as embodied in *ganguro* or *yamanba* girls, that *gyaru* culture was appreciated by many feminists in Japan. The girls' fashion and lifestyle were seen as an image of free, powerful women who resisted the traditional gender role expected in Japanese society. Mitsu Tanaka, the well-known activist and writer who led the women's liberation movement during the early 1970s in Japan, evaluates *gyaru* girls and 'their radical lifestyle' as heir to the spirit of *uuman ribu* (the women's liberation movement). Similarly, sociologist Kazue Muta (2001) appreciates the trend toward *gyaru* culture in the late 1990s as a form of feminist resistance to sexist ideals of feminine beauty. Muta regards gender performance by *ganguro* or *yamanba* girls as a 'practice of the very opposite of "cuteness" which has been expected for young women' and it is so brave of them to 'completely refuse to be looked as a "pleasant" woman' (2001, p. 201). Here, *gyaru* girls' self-expression is understood not just as a disregard for the male (or public) gaze but as an intentional and aggressive gesture of *refusing* it.

Even general interest publications such as the Japanese popular weekly magazine *AERA* covered feminist aspects of *gyaru* culture in 1999, representing *gyaru* fashion as a particular 'strategy' of gender performance with which to survive heterosexist society. The article quotes from interviews with *gyaru* girls, saying 'It's sort of like a self-modification' (*AERA*, 1999, p. 33), 'You are not *Gyaru* if you want the male approval' (*AERA*, 1999, p. 35), 'Transforming myself into a totally different person through flashy clothes and makeup. That's what I like' (*AERA*, 1999, p. 36). Here, too, the political potential of *gyaru* culture is understood as/through a strategic gender performance, depicted as not merely a masquerade but an even more aggressive armour, which is obviously the practice of the feminine but far from the normative.

Harajuku girls: *Kawaii* fashion for independent girls

If Shibuya was a 'home' for *gyaru* girls, Harajuku, more precisely the back street known as Ura-Harajuku, would certainly be another 'sacred place' for Japanese girls' culture. It is probably fair to say that today's notion of *kawaii* has its roots in Harajuku and has been developed there since the early 1990s. It is not about normative standards of beauty but is rather particular aesthetics which aim to deviate from or even reverse those standards (Koga, 2009, p. 210). Reiko Koga defines the *kawaii* fashion of Harajuku style as 'the fashion style which longs for something anarchic and weird' (2009, p. 80), while typical Harajuku girls' fashions are often described in terms such as 'mix-and-match', 'kitsch', 'anarchic' or 'punk'.

Harajuku girls dress up 'in brightly coloured prints and a tremendous load of accessories such as necklaces, plastic beads, and bracelets, many of which were handmade' (Macias and Evers, 2007, p. 133), or 'in a mismatch coordination such as vintage sweat jacket with a frilly tutu, a toy tiara on the head' (Koga, 2009, p. 81). 'Although it might appear just random', Koga points out, 'such fashion styles have been conventionalised with their [Harajuku girls'] *individualistic sense of "kawaii"* ' (2009, p. 81; my emphasis). Examples of Harajuku girls' outfits can be seen in Figures 7.1 and 7.2

As in the case of *gyaru* culture, the *kawaii* fashion of Harajuku girls has also aimed at establishing the girls' own style by intentionally deviating from mainstream culture and standardized fashion as much as possible. What happened there can be understood as an attempt

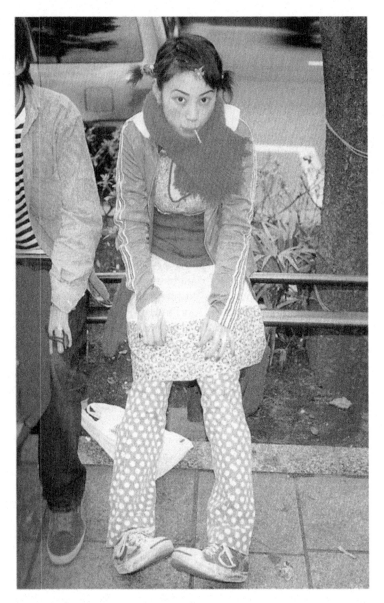

Figure 7.1 Harajuku girls' style from FRUiTS Year Book 1997 vol. 01 (2013), p. 108

Figure 7.2 Harajuku girls' style from FRUiTS Year Book 1997 vol. 01 (2013), p. 149

to reappropriate the dominant ideas of 'cuteness' which are fully contaminated with heterosexist assumptions, and it was precisely a *transformation* of existing images and meanings of the feminine.

For example, the fashion magazine *CUTiE* (1989–), which has gained overwhelming support from teenage girls especially since the mid-1990s, serves to rescue the meaning of cuteness from the male gaze and redefine it as a tool of self-expression for themselves. With the catchphrase 'for independent girls' on the cover, *CUTiE* featured female models who in male eyes, were 'not cute enough at all' (Koga, 2009, pp. 80–81), and presented the cutting-edge and revolutionary fashion style of the Harajuku back streets as a mode 'of the girls, by the girls, for the girls' (Koga, 2009, p. 126). Such sprit of independence that *CUTiE* put forward played a significant role in 'liberating' the notion of *kawaii* from the normative values of femininities which have been dominated by the male gaze in Japanese society.

In addition to the independent sprits of *kawaii* fashion among Harajuku girls, it is suggestive that Koga gives insights into the feeling of firm solidarity among the girls that has been generated through reform of the concept of *kawaii*. This sense of *kawaii* was supported by the individualistic desire to express oneself without being bothered by heterosexist expectations of the feminine, but simultaneously by 'the communication among the girls based on the strong feeling of "only *we* understand this style" ' (Koga, 2009, p. 136; my emphasis). As *gyaru* culture resists the normative image of femininity by fiercely exaggerating it, the political potential of *kawaii* fashion among Harajuku girls might lie in their attempts to transform what cuteness means and to create an alternative way to enjoy embodying femininities for no-one but themselves.

Reinvention of *kawaii* and commercialization of girls' culture

Since the late 2000s, the evaluation of Japanese girls' culture has drastically changed; their deviance from conventional norms of the feminine gender is no longer the object of criticism or derision, but on the contrary, is now a feature of the extraordinary uniqueness Japan should be proud of. By re-importing the word *kawaii*, suggesting consumption of Japanese girls' culture in the Euro-American context, the Japanese mainstream media reports that this culture has now become a representative product of the Japanese cultural industry like manga or anime, and emphasizes that it is now attracting the enthusiastic attention of the world. For example, NHK, Japan's national public broadcasting organization, in 2008 launched an information programme called 'Tokyo Kawaii TV'. The programme targets young women in Japan as its primary audience, and introduces whatever is hot, or *kawaii* as its title indicates, among the youth, particularly in Shibuya or Harajuku. What makes this programme interesting is the way it introduces Japanese girls' culture to an audience of girls in Japan, not merely as the trend but as a phenomenon unique enough to attract worldwide attention. Furthermore, these *kawaii* cultures have now played a significant role in Japan's national strategy. In 2009, the country's Ministry of Foreign Affairs officially appointed three women as 'Kawaii Taishi' (ambassadors of cuteness), to display particular genres of dress representing Japanese *kawaii*, such as the Lolita fashion or school girl uniform, and sent them overseas to promote the pop culture of 'Cool Japan' (The Press Secretary of MOFA, 2009).

Japanese girls' culture has become one of the flagship products of Japan's pop culture diplomacy, and the uniqueness of their feminine gender performance is celebrated for another (but mutually related, as we shall see shortly) desirable quality: flexibility. Recent re-evaluation of girls' culture largely owed to that culture's ability to create a positive economic impact by flexibly responding to changing market needs. What we cannot overlook here is that such economic flexibility is visualized through, and intricately linked (in both figurative and literal meanings) to, the culture's expression of the feminine gender performed by female bodies.

BRUTUS, a popular magazine published in Japan whose targeted reader is the 'metropolitan adult male' within a wide age range, provides a striking example of this re-evaluation and reinvention of Japanese girls' culture. In 2009, *BRUTUS* released a feature issue with the title 'Girls' Culture: Gyaru Saves Japan!?', showing how nationalistic discourses on Japanese girls' culture are connected to neoliberal economics in Japan. That culture is depicted as not merely something 'unique' but as 'flexible' enough to bring an innovative breakthrough to the Japanese economy in the midst of a protracted slump.

The issue begins with an article entitled 'The genealogy of Gyaru culture and Japanese economy' which reviews the historical changes in girls' culture by direct comparison with Japan's economic transition over the last 40 years (*BRUTUS*, 2009, pp. 18–19). This article defines a *gyaru* as 'a powerful girl who is capable of creating new styles', and emphasizes the capacity to adapt to the economic crisis and contribute to the reconstruction of the Japanese economy, with illustrations of girls who flexibly change their fashion and lifestyle. The article features some girls who have succeeded not only as models but also as leaders of the fashion industry, with comments from male critics praising the girls' flexibility in responding to rapid market changes and producing remarkable economic outcomes (*BRUTUS*, 2009, pp. 22–31). Economic analyst Takuro Morinaga, for example, points out *gyaru* culture's characteristic in its 'warp speed and sensitivity', stressing the ultrafast turnover time in *gyaru* markets (*BRUTUS*, 2009, pp. 20–21). In terms of flexibility, these descriptions of Japanese girls' culture are remarkably coincidental with characteristics which mark the post-Fordist neoliberal economic system. In contrast with the Fordist regime, which largely depended on mass production and mass consumption and was defined by rigidity or stability, the post-Fordist economic system has been captured by its flexible nature which allows it to adopt to the crisis of capitalism (McDonald, 1991, p. 181), and the turnover time in consumption has become shorter and shorter, along with a greater range of market needs which has become more specialized and individualized (Harvey, 1990, p. 156). Throughout the issue, *BRUTUS* illustrates the economic impact of the girls' culture by overlaying it with the visual image of their flexible performance of femininity.

Flexible 'n' quirky: Kyary Pamyu Pamyu and her unusual world of *kawaii*

What we need to draw critical attention to, then, is the way in which a certain type of femininity and female body are regarded as flexible enough to protest against or enhance socially dominant discourses. Kyary Pamyu Pamyu, a Japanese model, blogger and pop singer who has been hugely successful both in Japan and abroad, serves as an interesting example of the tangled power structure accommodating the politics of the flexible body.

Not long after Kyary Pamyu Pamyu made her debut as a pop singer in 2011, her debut song PonPonPon and its unusual music video became a huge hit not only in Japan but also around the world, through being uploaded to YouTube. Katy Perry mentioned that she was a huge fan of Kyary and introduced the music video PonPonPon on Twitter; since then it has been viewed more than 50 million times. In response to her popularity abroad, Kyary made her first global tour in 2013. She also graced the cover of *Dazed & Confused*, a British style magazine which featured her as the latest J-pop icon, leading and representing Asian youth culture (Jones, 2012). Even the BBC played up Kyary's global success, and she was featured as 'the face and the voice in Japan's "kawaii" or "cute" culture', the emphasis being on 'her reinvention of "kawaii" culture' as 'quirky' but quite catchy enough to attract worldwide attention (Oi, 2013).

On the one hand, Kyary's unusual self-expression largely shares the style of *gyaru* girls' 'self-modification' through non-normative fashion, and Harajuku girls' transformation of conventional values of beauty or cuteness into their own ('independent') sense of *kawaii*. At the same time, however, we need to be careful about why such a particular mode of femininity has recently been embraced, and how it is mobilized to sustain the normative, paradoxically, precisely because of its non-normative appearance. Kyary Pamyu Pamyu and her representation will serve as a case study through which to understand today's body politics of alternative femininity placed in the middle of the intricate power structure of neoliberalism, Orientalism and nationalism. I shall illuminate the way in which bodily flexibility as a desirable quality is achieved, as both consuming and consumable image of 'otherness', through focusing on some factors comprise *kawaii* in the representation of Kyary Pamyu Pamyu: flexibility, quirkiness and immaturity.

Kyary's flexible bodies: Theatricality, impersonation and transformation

One of the most prominent features of Kyary's *kawaii* can be found in its theatricality. Although Kyary's gender expression is not accompanied by gender-crossing, but instead is represented as obviously feminine ('cute'), her gender performance is certainly intended to be received as performance. When the particular mode of femininity known as *kawaii* is embodied, what is repeatedly emphasized is that *kawaii* is a theatrical effect which can be flexibly changed rather than being fixed in a 'natural' or unchangeable 'essence'. Such theatricality of Kyary's flexible body emerges best in her music video and in the songs written by her producer Yasutaka Nakata. While Kyary's music style is often characterized by catchy but meaningless lyrics, they are not random but provide an indispensable apparatus that cleverly functions to stage the *kawaii* through flexible bodies.

In her music videos, *kawaii* has been quite intentionally evoked through emphasis on its artificial, unreal and fantastic nature. While one of her songs 'Tsukema Tsukeru' (2012), literally meaning 'putting on fake eyelashes', is often mentioned as a typical example of lyrics which are 'annoyingly catchy' but 'don't make grammatical sense' (Oi, 2013), this song is far from meaningless; in fact it obviously and significantly represents the point of Kyary's theatrical world, *transformation*. In the music video, Kyary and two male backing dancers in lion suits 'transform' themselves into new costumes by pulling masks off and putting fake eyelashes on. Since what we see, when the dancer pulls off his lion mask, is another masked face instead of his naked face, the act of pulling off a mask here is not meant to reveal a 'true' self; rather what is emphasized in this video is the nature of *kawaii* which is always already performance, or as we might say, impersonation of impersonation. The lyrics of 'Tsukema Tsukeru' also conveys the concept of *kawaii*; it is a magical transformation which enables girls to be confident in themselves through practising masquerade and continuing to be (or impersonate) someone else rather than aspiring to the fiction of the true self.

What we need to articulate, then, is how such an image of *kawaii* as that which Kyary embodies is actually distributed in today's Japanese society and how such theatrical flexibility, as an essential component of *kawaii*, functions there. I shall look at Kyary's song 'Kyary ANAN' (2012) and illustrate how her flexible – and at the same time quite gendered – body has been mobilized in direct relationship with today's neoliberal capitalism.

'Kyary ANAN' was created as a tie-in song with a recruitment company Intelligence, Ltd., and released at the beginning of 2012 in the form of a TV commercial sound track for *AN*, a popular part-time job information magazine published by the company. In the commercial video, entitled 'Kyary Shichihenge' (Kyary in seven transformations), Kyary Pamyu Pamyu quickly changes into different costumes for various jobs, from road crew to cute waitress, one after another, while dancing to the up-tempo tune of 'Kyary ANAN'. What is depicted here is, again, a flexible body with the capacity for speedy transformation, and this flexible *and* gendered body performed by Kyary successfully functions so as to promote the commercial's theme; it corresponds to Japan's situation of an ever-growing irregular employment rate, or in other words, to expansion of the 'flexible' labour force which is also obviously gendered.

As shown by the latest result of the Labour Force Survey conducted by the Statistics Bureau of Japan, the increase in the rate of irregular employment is a serious problem in Japan today; 36.2% of workers, the highest rate ever recorded, are non-regular employees, with little or no job security or insurance coverage and on quite low wages (*Labour Force Survey in 2013 (Statistical Tables)* 2013b). Furthermore, the situation for female workers is even more severe. According to the same survey conducted in 2012, a startling 54.5% of female workers were irregular employees (*Labour Force Survey (2012 Yearly Average Result)* 2013a), which was also the highest rate ever recorded and is expected to grow. Such an increasing use of flexible labour, as David Harvey (1990) points out, enables firms to change the size of the workforce freely and quickly by firing or hiring workers in response to rapidly shifting market needs, thus achieving the ideal condition of flexibility in this neoliberal age. It is no coincidence, then, that Kyary Pamyu Pamyu has been chosen to perform the commercial for a part-time job magazine; not only on a symbolic level but also in quite a literal sense, the bodily flexibility which Kyary visualizes in her feminine gender performance functions to mobilize female workers as a flexible – that is cheap and dispensable – labour force.

Coupled with flexibility in the production process achieved by growth in the numbers of such flexible workers, we can see that the song 'Kyary ANAN' also represents flexibility in the mode of consumption as well. Like her other songs, 'Kyary ANAN' is characterized by its unusual catchy melody with repeated meaningless onomatope; however, the following lyrics of this song should not be ignored:

> Bokura wa hataraku yo yumemite
> (We work with dreams in our hearts)
> Kyou mo ashita mo baito ganbarou ne
> (We work part-time, let's enjoy working together)
> Are mo kore mo hoshii hatarako
> (We want this and that, so let's work)
> Konshuu mo raishuu mo ganbarou ne
> (This week and the following, let's work hard)

As these lyrics show, the bearer of Japanese pop culture is expected not only to be a flexible worker in the production process ('We work part-time, let's enjoy working together'), but at the same time to be a good customer at the level of consumption ('we want this and that, *so* let's work'). Beneath the guise of the flashy, playful and free images of Kyary's gender performance, female bodies are now required to be both consuming subjects *and* consumable (namely, 'dispensable') objects for achieving the neoliberal ideal of flexibility in the labour force.

Quirky enough to be flexible: The fetishization of otherness

How can it be possible, then, for Kyary Pamyu Pamyu, as the representative of *kawaii*, to attain such a desirable (even idealized) status with regard to flexibility? The question here is what kinds of images are called up and deployed to make Kyary's body flexible enough. Now, we might return to Biddy Martin's argument which reveals how bodily flexibility always demands visibility as such, namely, to be *visibly different* from norms (1996, p. 74). By applying Martin's insight on the problematic complicity between flexibility and visibility, I shall now shed light on the 'distancing effects' of Kyary's strategy of visibility, which constitutes another integral component of her *kawaii* performance, namely, mobilization of quirkiness.

As seen in most of the media coverage of Kyary Pamyu Pamyu, something strange or 'quirky' certainly serves to make her *kawaii* world different and remarkable. Describing it as 'quirky Kyary-ism', the BBC introduces Kyary and Japanese *kawaii* culture as follows:

> The 'kawaii' or 'cute' culture used to be about Hello Kitty, or schoolgirls obsessed with making their eyes look bigger like Barbie dolls. Kyary has been pushing the boundaries by *embracing the quirky* as part of her cute image.
>
> (BBC News, 2013; my emphasis)

As an example of Kyary's adoption of the quirky or even the grotesque, the BBC features eccentric motifs used in the music video of her debut song 'PonPonPon', such as 'children's toys, a dancing brain, a psychedelic shark' or 'skulls and dinosaurs spin around Kyary as bats and eyeballs fly out of her mouth' (Oi, 2013). With the caption 'The cute "n" kooky world of Kyary Pamyu Pamyu, Japan's new pop idol' accompanying a picture of the singer dressed in hundreds of teddy bears, *The Japan Times* similarly stresses how unique her 'visual philosophy' of cuteness is: Kyary's distinctive aesthetics lie in the act of 'twisting meanings'; her *kawaii* world is constructed by exaggerating something cute to such 'an extreme that it becomes uncomfortable', and at the same time, by discovering 'cute aspects inside things you wouldn't generally think of in that way' (Martin, 2011).

It seems obvious that the pronounced visuality/visibility of the quirky functions to allow her feminine gender performance of *kawaii* to be visible as flexible despite a lack of gender crossing. What we need to call into question, then, is what specific types of images are adopted and deployed as the quirky; or, more precisely, whose bodies are mobilized to establish Kyary's visibly flexible body. Rather than flying colourful eyeballs or dancing pink brains, I shall draw attention again to the bodies of her backing dancers, who make up a significant part of the *mise en scène* of Kyary's *kawaii* world.

Let us consider what kinds of bodies have been represented as 'the quirky' and adopted into Kyary's visual philosophy of the *kawaii* world, by tracing her music videos from her song 'PonPonPon', released in 2011. Here, the body of a black-faced, fat, female dancer is effectively appropriated and (ab)used to stage Kyary's quirkiness. In a sharp contrast to the pink frilled dress and white wig that the dancer wears, her blacked-out face is emphasized by video editing, as a result of which her body can also be seen as a stereotyped image of a 'black mammy'.

'Tsukema Tsukeru' (2012), the song mentioned above, foregrounds the bodies of backing dancers even more blatantly. In the middle of the song, we can see two dancers in lion suits, performing dynamic choreography, whereupon effeminized male bodies appear out of the lion suits. In addition to the costume of those half-naked dancers, featuring pink and lavender-coloured bras and fox masks (with, of course, fake eyelashes), the choreography also serves to emphasize a certain femininity of their bodies. What is evoked as the quirky here is obviously a stereotyped image of the *onee* character, the Japanese media representation of the effeminized male (including, but not exclusive to gay and/or MtF transgender people).

In the video of her second single 'Candy Candy' (2012), a cross-gender figure of a backing dancer is mobilized to provide a vivid contrast with Kyary. The quirky part of Kyary's performance is achieved through the body of a male dancer whose costume is exactly the same as hers. The dancer's mask, representing the face of a typical girl character in Japanese manga/animation, together with the powerful choreography of this song, also helps to highlight the incongruous contrast between the dancer's male body and his costume, representing the cross-dressed body as the 'unnatural'.

What all these music videos of Kyary Pamyu Pamyu have in common is the obscuring of the backing dancers' faces by masks or video editing, which functions to emphasize the visuality of *their* bodies' quirkiness, as well as to embody the theatrical character of the *kawaii* performance. It is the 'otherness' of those backing dancers' bodies – not that of Kyary's own body – that the music videos consistently present as quirky. Through mobilizing these body images of the 'other', Kyary's feminine gender performance is allowed to be visible as the flexible, Japanese-embodying, innovative *kawaii* culture without either being marked with the sign of 'otherness' or being invisible. Kyary's 'visual philosophy' is, despite its appearance, far from 'twisting meanings', but is rather based on the imposition of otherness on certain bodies; her unique *kawaii* performance becomes possible only at the expense of those other (marked/visible) bodies.

This is exactly what Carol-Anne Tyler (2003) calls the 'distancing effects' of female impersonation or drag. Pointing out 'the potentially oppressive effects of mimicry or drag', Tyler lucidly draws attention to the mechanism by which the ironic gender performance is made legible as – or visible as – 'an obvious fake' (2003, p. 102). Drag or female impersonation requires that it *not* be conflated with the 'real thing', and the ironic distance between them is all too often maintained by exploiting the excess of the other, or more precisely, by constituting 'the other as what must be repudiated' (2003, p. 105). Tyler's insight into the 'distancing effects' of female impersonation, which is achieved through 'a disidentification that takes the form of an apparent identification' (2003, p. 105) with 'other' bodies, is highly suggestive for understanding Kyary's apparent embracement of the quirky. The flexibility of Kyary's *kawaii* performance can be visible only through the deployment, disguised as endorsement, of the bodies of the fetishized 'other', by sustaining or even reinforcing the normative/oppressive ideas of racial, sexual and physical differences which are taken for granted as 'the non-normative' (thus 'quirky' or 'grotesque') in Japanese society.

Furthermore, it should also be noted that Kyary's strategy of visibility has recently undergone drastic change. In the face of growing worldwide attention, the visibility of Kyary's quirky *kawaii* performance has been increasingly achieved through the Orientalized image of Japan; quirkiness is transferred from the 'other' bodies to Kyary's own body dressed in a kimono or ninja costume, which embodies the familiar stereotype of exotic Japan. For instance, the music video of 'Furisodation' (2013) features, as the title indicates, 'Furisode', a style of kimono which is normally worn by unmarried women at the coming-of-age ceremony in Japan. Using basic tones of red and white – the colour combination traditionally used for the celebration, but also recalling the Japanese flag – this video adopts the motif of 'Origami' for the dancers' costumes. The old-fashioned cliché of Japanese-ness is similarly reproduced in her music video 'Ninja Re Bang Bang' (2013), in which we see Kyary Pamyu Pamyu dressed in a ninja costume, dancing with animated robot characters whose movements are choreographed in *kabuki* style.

It is all too obvious that this employment of an Orientalized image of Japanese-ness in Kyary's current performances is intended to appeal to global (which means, presumably, mostly Euro-American) audiences, and such a shift in the target audience modifies her strategy of visibility. Kyary's flexible body, which has exploited the fetishized 'other' body, now also comes to be exploited – as the 'other' body of the exotic Asian female – responding to the Western gaze towards Japan and reinforcing the Oriental image of eccentric but/thus attractive Japanese-ness. This problematical linkage between 'the quirky' and the Orientalized image of Japanese-ness may be compatible with another component of Kyary's *kawaii* performance, namely, *immaturity*.

Kyary's immaturity and *kawaii* nationalism

Lastly, I shall briefly describe how Kyary' s espousal of the quirky functions to establish nationality by translating it into 'Japanese uniqueness' which 'we' must be proud of, while connecting her performance to the negative notion of 'immaturity' which constitutes a prominent nature of *kawaii* culture. In collusion with fetishistic/Orientalistic mobilization of the quirky, Kyary's *kawaii* performance also emerges as an image of immaturity that not only serves to signify 'otherness' but paradoxically builds up the discourses of Japanese nationalism.

To determine the particular context in which Kyary's strategy of immaturity is celebrated as intrinsic Japanese-ness, it might be indicative to compare it to another representation of the flexible body, namely, that of Lady Gaga. Kyary Pamyu Pamyu is often compared to Lady Gaga, with the emphasis on their similarity in terms of unusual fashion sense (Oi, 2013). I agree that they apparently have something in common as regards flexible bodily performance; however, their tactics of visualization of/through the non-normative, which enable them to appear as the flexible, take precisely opposite directions. On the one hand, Gaga's strategy of bodily flexibility and its huge success should be understood not only in the context of US homonormativity but also through the phenomenon of US homonationalism. As a 'gay icon' or LGBT-friendly artist, Lady Gaga has quite intentionally and cleverly incorporated sexual (and other) minority communities into her unusual and flexible performance, which thus serves not only to commercialize and depoliticize gay culture (Duggan, 2003, p. 50) but also to facilitate a homonationalistic discourse of 'U.S. sexual exceptionalism' (Puar, 2007), establishing the US as 'a properly multicultural heteronormative but nevertheless gay-friendly, tolerant, and sexually liberated society' (Puar, 2007, p. 39). This is exactly the context in which her song 'Born This Way' (2011) became a smash hit with her celebration of difference and diversity; the song reveals how Gaga's 'constant fluidity of identities' (Leibetseder, 2012, p. 77), and her image as 'the first subversive queer role model in mainstream pop' (Leibetseder, 2012, p. 78) are strongly connected to an idealized image of the United States as a 'liberated', 'progressive' and thus 'mature' nation.[3]

By contrast, Kyary Pamyu Pamyu's unusual and flexible body projects negative concepts such as 'immaturity' or 'imperfection', and nevertheless it is oddly bound to the nationalistic discourses of Japan. It seems pertinent to say that 'if Gaga was a symbol of the queer, Kyary would be a symbol of the weird' (*Soushokukei Danshi*, 2011), Kyary's embodiment of the *kawaii* and its quirkiness win domestic praise precisely because she perfectly embodies Japan's potential for immaturity. Yasutaka Nakata, Japanese songwriter and Kyary's music producer, explains, in a BBC interview, how her *kawaii* fashion and the catchy music he composes for her are 'full of deviation from the norm':

> 'What is different about Kyary is that she is not afraid to be uncool,' Mr Nakata says. . . . But these *imperfections*, according to J-Pop's young mastermind, are what the kawaii culture is about. 'I think it derives from *our own inferiority complexes*, so we try to treat our *shortcomings as positive* by making them cute,' he said.
>
> (Oi, 2013; my emphasis)

Here, with Nakata referring to '*our own* inferiority complexes' and '*our* shortcomings', Kyary and her *kawaii* fashion are mobilized to create a direct link between inferiority and Japanese nationality.[4] By contrast with Lady Gaga's celebration of progress or maturity, feelings of national inferiority are expressed as 'the immature' or 'the infantile'. Depicting the clear linkage among the infantile, inferiority, cuteness and Japanese-ness, Nakata explains how his own works are inspired by *kawaii* culture; 'For example, if a child is playing piano badly, that's cute. I am trying to create that imperfection with my music' (Oi, 2013). It might not be far-fetched to believe, then, that Kyary's employment of a children's dance group, TEMPURA KIDS, as her backing dancers effectively serves to dramatize the immaturity of her *kawaii* performance. It is the children's bodies that are mobilized to provide an images of immaturity, but at the same time, they also emphasize the imperfection of Kyary's dancing body, which is executing fairly dull movements, in contrast to the well-trained, dynamic dancing bodies of the children.

What is happening here is nothing less than complicity between Orientalism and nationalism; this strategic incorporation of an Orientalized image of Japanese inferiority/immaturity, which simultaneously constructs the West as progressive and mature, should be questioned not simply because it naïvely enforces the old-fashioned (but deep-rooted) East–West dichotomy. Rather, it would be even more problematic precisely because of its intentionality to adopt such an Orientalist image of Japan as immature, for the reason that it also builds up national identity by mobilizing the figures of femininity, without questioning its connection with inferiority/

immaturity. We should not overlook that this dramatic sublimation of the negative (Japanese inferiority/immaturity) into the positive (Japanese uniqueness), which is accompanied by circulation of the *kawaii* images, requires femininity itself to remain inferior and immature. Just as Kyary's *kawaii* performance achieves its status as the quirky by mobilizing figures of the 'other' bodies, it is now Kyary's body that is mobilized as a signifier of immaturity to erect so-called Japanese-ness as unique and even 'better' in comparison to the straightforward narrative of maturity on which the West often depends. In other words, in the guise of identification with the immature, such reappropriation or recontextualization of the negative image of Japan can only be achieved by misogynistic assumption of the feminine which is 'really' inferior and immature.

Although some theorists of Japanese pop culture tend to celebrate such (deliberate) reappropriation of Japanese immaturity by *kawaii* culture, in terms of its political potential to deconstruct or subvert the (hetero)normative aspiration towards progress or maturity (Vincent, 2010), the problematic power structure surrounding Kyary Pamyu Pamyu's flexible gender performance is blatantly obvious. Today's celebration of the image of Kyary's flexible, quirky and immature performance shares a strong affinity with the (re)import and export of the *kawaii* culture as a diplomatic tool of Japan. The worldwide and domestic admiration for Kyary Pamyu Pamyu and the *kawaii* culture she embodies has to be understood within the complicated intersection of neoliberalism, Orientalism and nationalism: at the same time unreserved celebration of the *kawaii* phenomenon as representing the possibility of flexible femininity could help to enforce the oppressive logic on which it stands

Notes

1. Macias and Evers emphasise how *gyaru* girls became the target of misogynous bashing by the media at that moment, introducing the interview with *gyaru* girl: 'The media wanted to depict us as "dirty girls", said Mizuno, which was totally not true.... Then there were lies that we were prostitutes, that we had AIDS' (2007, p. 64).
2. Macias and Evers cite the example of Buriteri, one of the most charismatic *gyaru* girls at the time, who was forced to give up the *gonguro* fashion by the negative press and public pressure: 'I'd just be sitting down somewhere

and an adult would come along and point at me, screaming out stuff like "cockroach", or "How sickening!"' (2007, pp. 64–66).
3. It should not be overlooked, as Kazuyoshi Kawasaka points out, that today's 'globalisation' of sexual politics all too often means 'Americanisation' of LGBT politics; it would be no coincidence that Gaga's 'Born This Way' and her celebration of sexual minorities in the song became a huge (and 'global') hit in the exactly same year when Hillary Clinton gave an historical speech about same-sex marriage in the US, declaring that 'gay rights are human rights' (Kawasaka, 2013).
4. In the Japanese version of the same article, we can see that Nakata responds to the interviewer by literally saying 'inferiority complexes that *Japanese people* have'. See Oi, M. (2013) 'J-pop to sekaiteki ninki no "kawaii" bunka' ['J-pop and the global success of "kawaii" culture'], *BBC World News*. London: BBC. Available from: http://www.bbcworldnews-japan.com/uk _topics/view/0000217> (Accessed: 27 October 2013).

Bibliography

BBC News (2013) 'Japanese singer Kyary Pamyu Pamyu talks instant stardom', BBC, 4 June. Available online at: http://www.bbc.co.uk/news/world-asia -22762974 (accessed 26 October 2013).

Brown, J. (2011) 'Re-framing "Kawaii": Interrogating global anxieties surrounding the aesthetic of "cute" in Japanese art and consumer products', *The International Journal of the Image*, 1(2), pp. 1–10.

Brutus (1 May 2009) Tokyo: Magazine House.

Butler, J. (1990) *Gender Trouble: Feminism and the Subversion of Identity*. New York and London: Routledge.

Duggan, L. (2003) *The Twilight of Equality?: Neoliberalism, Cultural Politics, and the Attack on Democracy*. Boston: Beacon Press.

Genz, Stéphenie. and Benjamin. A. Bradon, (2009) *Postfeminism: Cultural Texts and Theories*. Edinburgh: Edinburgh University Press, pp. 76–90.

Haberstam, J. (2005) *In a Queer Time and Place: Transgender Bodies, Subcultural Lives*. New York and London: New York University Press.

Harvey, D. (1990) *The Condition of Postmodernity*. Oxford: Blackwell.

AERA (15 November 1999) 'Iatsu gyaru no honne: Otoko wo mushi shita busou fassyon' ['Truth talk of intimidating gyaru: Arming fashion in ignoring the guy'], pp. 32–36.

Holland, Samantha and Julie Harpin (2013) 'Who is the "girly" girl?: Tomboys, hyperfemininity and gender', *Journal of Gender Studies*. pp. 1–17.

Jones, Charlie Rorbin. (2012) 'Kyary Pamyu Pamyu covershoot: The PonPonPon has a laugh with Nicola behind the scenes of her Dazed covershoot', *Dazed Digital*. London: Waddell Limited. Available online at: http://www.dazeddigital.com/fashion/article/15088/1/kyary -pamyu-pamyu-covershoot (accessed 25 October 2013).

Kawasaka, Kazuyoshi (2013) 'Are LGBT rights becoming Americanised?' *(Im)possibly Queer International Feminisms: Second Annual International*

Feminist Journal of Politics Conference. Brighton: University of Sussex, pp. 17–19.

Keet, Philomena. (2007) *The Tokyo Look Book: Stylish to Spectacular, Goth to Gyaru, Sidewalk to Catwalk.* Tokyo, New York and London: Kodansha International.

Leibetseder, Doris. (2012) *Queer Tracks: Subversive Strategies in Rock and Pop Music.* Surrey and Burlington: Ashgate.

Macias, Patrick and Evers, Izumi (2007) *Japanese Schoolgirl Inferno: Tokyo Teen Fashion Subculture Handbook.* San Francisco: Chronicle Books LLC.

Martin, Biddy. (1996) 'Sexualities without genders and other queer Utopias', *Femininity Played Straight: The Significance of Being Lesbian.* New York and London: Routledge.

Martin, Emily. (1994) *Flexible Bodies: The Role of Immunity in American Culture from the Days of Polio to the Age of AIDS.* Boston: Beacon Press.

Martin, Ian. (2011) 'The cute 'n' kooky world of Kyary Pamyu Pamyu, Japan's newest pop idol', *The Japan Times.* Tokyo: The Japan Times, Ltd. Available online at: http://www.japantimes.co.jp/culture/2011/09/29/culture/the-cute-n-kooky-world-of-kyary-pamyu-pamyu-japans-newest-pop-idol/#.Umuph46jrfv (accessed 24 October 2013).

McRuer, Robert. (2006) *Crip Theory: Cultural Signs of Queerness and Disability.* New York and London: New York University Press.

Murnen, Sarah K. and Byrne, Donn (1991) 'Hyperfemininity: Measurement and initial validation of the construct', *The Journal of Sex Research,* 28(3), p. 479.

Muta, Kazue. (2001) 'Bai-bai shun to enjo kosai', *Jissen suru feminizumu* ['Prostitution and compensated dating'], *Feminism in Practice.* Tokyo: Iwanami Shoten.

Ngai, Sianne. (2005) 'The cuteness of the Avant-Garde', *Critical Inquiry,* 31(4), pp. 811–847.

Oi, Mariko. (2013) 'J-Pop and the global success of "kawaii" culture', *BBC Worldwide.* London: BBC. Available online at: http://www.bbc.com/culture/story/20130603-cute-culture-and-catchy-pop (accessed 6 August 2013).

Oi, Mariko. (2013) 'J-pop to sekaiteki ninki no "kawaii" bunka' ['J-pop and the global success of "kawaii" culture'], *BBC World News.* London: BBC. Available online at: http://www.bbcworldnews-japan.com/uk_topics/view/0000217 (accessed 27 October 2013).

Puar, Jasbir K. (2007) *Terrorist Assemblages: Homonationalism in Queer Times.* Durham and London: Duke University Press.

'Soro soro Kyary Pamyu Pamyu ni tsuite hitokoto ittokimasuka', *Soushokukei Danshi.* (2011) Available online at: http://masafiro1986.blogspot.jp/2011/10/blog-post_11.html (accessed 24 October 2013).

Statistics Bureau of Japan, Ministry of Internal Affairs and Communications (2013a) *Roudouryoku chousa (Heisei 24-nen heikin kekka no gaiyou)* [*Labour Force Survey (2012 Yearly Average Result)*]. Tokyo: Statistics Bureau, Ministry of Internal Affairs and Communications. Available online at: http://www.stat.go.jp/data/roudou/sokuhou/nen/dt/pdf/ndtindex.pdf (accessed 16 October 2013).

Statistics Bureau of Japan, Ministry of Internal Affairs and Communications (2013b) *Roudouryoku chousa (Heisei 25-nen 4–6 gatsuki heikin (sokuhou) kekka no gaiyou)* [*Labour Force Survey in 2013 (Statistical Tables)*]. Tokyo: Statistics Bureau, Ministry of Internal Affairs and Communications. Available online at: http://www.stat.go.jp/data/roudou/sokuhou/4hanki/dt/pdf/2013_2.pdf (accessed 16 October 2013).

Tanaka, Mitsu. (2005) 'Issai toshi wo gomakashite…Sorega watashi no genten nanoyo', *Kakegae no nai, taishita koto no nai watakushi*. Tokyo: Impact Shuppankai. ['Faking my age…That's Where I Started', *One and Only, But Small Me*. Tokyo: Impact Shuppankai].

Tasker, Yvonne and Diane Negra (2007) 'Introduction: Feminist politics and postfeminist culture', in Yvonne Tasker and Diane Negra (eds.) *Interrogating Postfeminism: Gender and the Politics of Popular Culture*. Durham and London: Duke University Press, pp. 1–25.

The Press Secretary of MOFA (2009) *Press Conference, 12 March 2009*. Tokyo: Ministry of Foreign Affairs. Available online at: http://www.mofa.go.jp/announce/press/2009/3/0312.html (accessed 1 December 2013).

Tyler, Carole-Anne. (2003) 'Boy will be girls: Drag and transvestic fehishsm', *Female Impersonation*. New York and London: Routledge.

Vincent, Keith. (2010) '"Nihonteki miseijuku" no keifu' ['Genealogy of Japanese immaturity'], in H. Azuma (eds.) *Nihonteki souzouryoku no mirai: Cool Japanology no kanousei* [*The Future of Japanese Imagination: The Potentiality of Cool Japanology*]. Tokyo: NHK Books.

8
'Whatever it is that you desire, halve it': The Compromising of Contemporary Femininities in Neo-Victorian Fictions

Karen Sturgeon-Dodsworth

Much has been written about the progressive nature of neo-Victorian fiction. The films and literature that comprise the genre have been championed by those feminist scholars and queer theorists who regard it as an effective means of revealing hidden histories, illuminating the problematic gender politics of the past and exposing the tyrannies of patriarchy. Indeed, the form could be considered uniquely well-suited to explorations of these issues and to an ongoing deconstruction of the tensions that exist between the past and present, regressive and progressive agendas, traditionalism and radicalism. One of the most notable aspects of neo-Victorian fiction is that many of its characters, whether they embody the constituent archetypes of the Victorian milieu or are manifestly resistant to them, provide opportunities to either decry traditionalism or vaunt radical femininities, new masculinities and a range of non-normative sexualities. In particular, the representations of femininities found in these fictions prove to be markedly more diverse and more complex than established Victorian stereotypes, with Roland Barthes's idea of the doxological Victorian increasingly questioned, challenged or critiqued through their progressive characteristics.[1] Jeanette King (2005) talks of neo-Victorianism as an 'opportunity to challenge the answers which nineteenth-century society produced in response to the "Woman Question"' and this challenge is widely acknowledged as a crucial facet of the genre (2005, p. 6).

These ideas are well documented and, notwithstanding the direction of travel below, I do not seek to deny the existence of such progressive representations. However, I do want to suggest that these positive elements risk masking a more problematic set of representations that co-exist alongside them and even bind to them. Indeed, I will argue here that many of the seemingly progressive twenty-first century femininities transposed onto the bold nineteenth-century characters in recent neo-Victorian fictions are, within narratives that superficially appear to valorize them, also undermined, compromised and effaced by highly troubling counter-energies: progressive shifts are undone by a recalcitrant spirit that sees outwardly progressive figures revert to their 'pre-ordained' place within the heterosexual matrix or submit to relative passivity. It is my assertion that through and in their New Women many contemporary neo-Victorian fictions fashion an entirely illusory radicalism, with a number of mainstream twenty-first century films and novels using the form and its expected representations of strong femininities to pay lip service to progressive gender ideals while never fully upholding them. These are neo-Victorian fictions that use the tropes of the genre to figure a more disturbing engagement with the past, validating retrograde ideology and reifying conservative ideals, while seeming to operate within the counter-hegemonic spirit of their antecedents.

An appropriate place to start in exploring these ideas is Guy Ritchie's mainstream appropriation of Arthur Conan Doyle's detective Sherlock Holmes. Ritchie's two neo-Victorian films epitomise a particular approach to the representation of progressive femininities, and the representational strategies he employs serve to reveal a disturbing trend in many recent neo-Victorian works. Both *Sherlock Holmes* (Guy Ritchie, 2009) and the sequel *Sherlock Holmes: A Game of Shadows* (Guy Ritchie, 2011) feature the character of Irene Adler, a figure who features in Arthur Conan Doyle's 'A Scandal in Bohemia' (Conan Doyle, 2012). Adler provides an especially telling example of the reinvention of a Victorian womanhood that can be readily transposed onto twenty-first century femininities and made identifiable, relatable and accessible to a contemporary audience. It is perhaps prudent then, to consider briefly how Adler is represented in the original source text. Here, she is portrayed to the reader as an unusually powerful and potent woman, one who defies many of the conventions traditionally associated with nineteenth-century womanhood. Conan Doyle underlines her status in the opening paragraphs in which he asserts that 'to Sherlock Holmes she is always *the* woman... in his eyes she eclipses and predominates the whole of her sex' (Conan Doyle, 2012, p. 139). This sense of Adler's potency is subsequently developed within a narrative in which she ensnares and controls powerful men. The King of Bohemia finds himself blackmailed by her, Holmes is outwitted by her, and, uniquely, she assumes the role of both agent of disequilibrium and resolution, facilitating the story's denouement where Holmes fails. In addition, Adler is comprised of a range of characteristics that the male characters cannot help but admire: while she remains overtly feminine she nonetheless embodies many attributes which at the time of writing would be considered masculine virtues – logic, conviction, intelligence and an uncompromising agency. The King of Bohemia states that 'she has the face of the most beautiful of women and the mind of the most resolute of men', confirming her ability to transcend conventional moral judgements and impress because of her difference (2012, p. 149). As such, Adler would appear to be a character who 'has it all', a figure ripe for filmic appropriation in as much as she embodies a twenty-first century femininity that is capable of striking a chord with modern audiences. One might imagine then, that her elevation from bit part player – appearing only briefly in the works of Conan Doyle – to lead female protagonist, might point to a celebration of her resonance within a postfeminist present. And at least superficially this would appear to be the case, but, as I shall argue here, there is a retrograde element to Ritchie's Adler that effaces her radical potential and points to worrying undercurrents within our contemporary postfeminist moment.

Initially, Ritchie's Adler is represented as a bold and transgressive figure. She is first seen among an otherwise entirely male crowd, witnessing Holmes engage in a bare-knuckle fight. Early intimations that she will become Holmes's love interest are suggested by the familiar trope of her initialled handkerchief placed at ringside for him to discover, yet this loaded signifier with its traditional connotations of romance and chivalry is somewhat undercut by her enjoyment of the fight and her participation in the spectacle. Subsequently, Adler's overt wink at Holmes – an almost lecherous acknowledgement of Downey Jnr's shirtless male object of desire – serves to position Adler as a modern woman, sexual, desirous, transgressive and, crucially, presented in marked contrast to the three women who precede her in the narrative. Earlier, Ritchie has presented us with the sacrificial damsel in distress laid out before the vampiric Lord Blackwood, wearing little more than a sheet of gauze; Mrs Hudson the maternal, chiding house keeper; and Mary, Watson's fiancé, fawning and besotted. When juxtaposed against these more traditional figures, Irene Adler seems markedly more progressive and instantly more akin to a twenty-first century woman. Far from shying away from the violence, as one would expect of a Victorian lady, Adler moves confidently among the baying crowd, placing bets and showing no sign of unease. Ritchie's mise-en-scène also underscores her confidence and independence: dressed entirely in red she cuts a vampish figure who stands out against an otherwise muted colour palette, her flawless complexion contrasting sharply against the florid faces of the men in the crowd. The black lining of her red coat, her crimson lipstick and her arch expression immediately establish her as a form of femme fatale, her calling card gaining Holmes's attention before she disappears from sight, tantalizing the male protagonist. Clearly this is a proactive woman in control, a woman for whom propriety and the moral standards of the time are incidental and a woman encoded as attractive *because* of her dynamic, transgressive and modern qualities.

A brief ellipsis and then Adler is introduced more fully – a synecdochal close-up of her hand cradling two walnuts before she crushes them implying that this woman is indeed a 'ballbreaker'. Having entered Holmes's sanctum while he was sleeping she then proceeds to dominate this masculine space, the sense of agency implied by this action subsequently supplemented as she recounts her travels to a furtive Holmes, reading through the file he keeps on her and thus furnishing the audience with further knowledge of her capabilities. We learn of Adler's many husbands, her ability to enrapture men, the riches they give her and her inevitable boredom with them. She is frequently framed on the left of the shot with a high eye line, occupying the dominant position in compositions that reinforce her power over an enervated Holmes. When she leaves she rights the photograph that Holmes, in his embarrassment, has surreptitiously turned face down to hide his evident infatuation. Here then, is a woman who is in control of the gaze, acknowledging her power to control that gaze, situating Holmes as one of many men to have become infatuated with her – a conquest – before leaving him to play the atonal chords on his violin that he uses to impose order onto chaos. This picture of Adler as the epitome of postfeminist woman is soon completed when, on exiting Baker Street, she is assaulted by two thugs posing as flower sellers. She is drawn to the red roses and the romance they connote, but then singled out as a victim because of the overt femininity apparent in both her bearing and her dress, she nevertheless soon incapacitates one assailant with a cosh hidden up her sleeve and holds a knife to the throat of the other, shaving off a section of his beard then taking both his money and the roses. Here, she is confirmed as a figure drawn to traditional feminine pleasures yet her femininity does not diminish her prowess – she is physically capable and the mise en scène of cosh and knife represent her as a potent phallic woman.

Viewed from our perspective in the contemporary moment, the character of Irene Adler seems imbued with those qualities most vaunted by a postfeminist present. She appears to be a free spirit with evident agency and absolute independence, a figure of great beauty who is yet respected and even feared for those qualities and strengths that do not fall within the sphere of traditional femininity. Stephanie Genz's ideas regarding postfeminism prove particularly pertinent when addressing these qualities and articulating Adler's status as a contemporary figure. Genz describes the postfeminist state in terms of forces that can be accessed and channelled simultaneously, with postfeminist woman existing between the two poles of femininity and feminism, yet able to move between each without forgoing the other. She situates postfeminist woman as one who can operate to reconcile contradictions, an active agent of synthesis who can exist as someone who 'has it all'. One only has to analyse the representation of Adler in the early scenes of the film to note her ability to embody a multi-faceted state: we see her ability to move freely between an overt femininity and an absolute strength, and might at this point reasonably see her as Genz's postfeminist woman par excellence, the woman who 'rearticulates and blurs the binary distinctions between feminism and femininity, between professionalism and domesticity, refuting monolithic and homogenous definitions of postfeminist subjectivity' (Genz, 2010, p. 98). In both Adler's ability to supersede the conventional femininities presented in Mary, Mrs Hudson and Blackwood's victim, and her willingness to cross boundaries and move independently with the assurance of a flâneur, these ideas ring true: she is defined only in terms of her indefinability and her adaptability. Tellingly, when describing the postfeminist woman, Genz has stated that

> armed with a feminist consciousness, she is alert to the tyranny of femininity that constructs the female subject as a passive object of male desire. Yet, simultaneously, she is also aware of her feminine power and its potential to be deployed in new and liberating ways.
>
> (Genz, 2010, p. 108)

Certainly Adler's performance in the first half of the film contains much that echoes these ideas and, crucially, her juxtaposition against the Victorian milieu makes these facets of character overt, conspicuous, hyperreal and, in a way that initially seems symptomatic of her progressive gender identity, markedly other.

Midway through *Sherlock Holmes*, Irene Adler appears to constitute an unassailably powerful image of femininity; however, all of Adler's progressive qualities are undermined within the narrative phases that follow. Firstly, she disappears from the narrative – her role as active agent is over and from this point on she will perform entirely more traditional narrative functions. When she reappears she is, in the words of the antagonist, a 'lamb to the slaughter', chained to a meat hook in an abattoir and heading towards flames and a bandsaw. In an unlikely narrative reversal she has become the damsel in distress, Holmes confirming her new passivity and need as he asks, 'In over your head darling?' Once rescued she slumps into his arms, fluttering her eyes, breathily whispering her thanks. Adler elects to flee the danger she is now in. Her change in character is encoded in the fact that the vibrant red she has worn hitherto in the narrative is now replaced with a dull blue tone that has her blend in to her surroundings. Gone is the confident, head-held-high swagger, instead she is furtive and fearful, revealing the preceding image of power as fake, at best a cool performance, and at worst an empty masquerade. Subsequently, when she boards her train to make her escape she is confronted by her shadowy male employer who asserts that she will leave when he permits her to do so. He reminds her that her role was to manipulate Holmes's feelings for her 'not succumb to them', information she receives with an abashed glance downwards, acknowledging the truth of his words. Adler is now a conventionally emotional, fragile woman: when she is told that if she fails again the next dead body will be that of Holmes she gasps in fear, reinforcing the notion that her retrogressive transformation is complete. She has become, in a form of narrative recapitulation that equates her to Blackwood's victim in the opening scene, a passive figure, controlled and enmeshed by powerful men and her emotional attachment to our male protagonist. She remains silent during her next two scenes, in which she passively watches as Holmes and Watson actively determine the course of the action.

The resolution of *Sherlock Holmes* stages Irene Adler's capitulation in miniature. Though never as assured as she is in the early part of the film she nonetheless momentarily reasserts her active role, dispatching henchmen and disarming a chemical weapon while Holmes and Watson pursue their markedly more active and dynamic struggles against a towering giant of an antagonist. As the film reaches its climactic moments, however, Adler is once again denuded of her agency. Pushed from Tower Bridge by Lord Blackwood, she remains unconscious as Holmes heroically brings about justice and narrative resolution. With Blackwood defeated Holmes looks to Adler, handcuffing her even as she weeps and confesses that her 'weakness' was Holmes himself.

If this eventual compromise were not enough, Adler's fate in the sequel provides an emphatic rebuttal of her power and agency before proceeding to replay this same narrative trajectory in the form of Madam Simza. In the opening moments of *Sherlock Holmes: Game of Shadows* Adler's skill, agency and autonomy are briefly reprised in a fight scene in which her physical daring and intelligence are momentarily showcased. However, this cameo appearance ends moments later with her kidnap and subsequent death at the hands of Moriarty. Adler becomes a conventional romantic figure after her death, a fond memory cherished by Holmes who vows to avenge her and from this point the narrative will confirm that Holmes/Watson possess the necessary strength and ingenuity to pass the test that Adler failed and bring about narrative resolution. Significantly, the narrative device of the strong woman eventually compromised is then played out in almost identical form through the character of the gypsy fortune-teller Madam Simza. Like Adler, Simza is represented early in the narrative in 'male' territory, telling fortunes in the side room of a gentleman's club and gambling den. Like Adler she is soon revealed as an active fighting force, breaking down the fragility of femininity stereotype in emphatic terms. However, at almost precisely the same point in the narrative as Adler is compromised in the first film, Simza, the strong woman, is betrayed by her femininity, weakened, and, on the verge of hysteria, told to 'calm down, take a deep breath' and to follow the capable, purposeful males out of the dire situation they find themselves in. During a subsequent scene in the Tuileries of Paris, Simza is extraordinarily passive, mute for minutes on end as Holmes and Watson plot and plan. By the end of the film Simza is completely feminized – wearing a ballgown, dancing with Holmes and proving herself to be another female character incorporated into a neo-Victorian text in order to espouse notions of modernity and appeal to female audiences, only to have her strong twenty-first century characteristics emphatically disavowed.

What emerges from this marked shift in both Adler's and Simza's characters is that their early strength and agency are little more than masquerade, far removed from any discernable agenda or consistent ideology. Even as these women appear to signify empowerment in truth they have no power when it truly counts. Pertinently, Joel Gwynne, quoting Christina Sharff, has noted that 'new feminisms do not sufficiently interrogate the social constellations that initially gave rise to the felt need for a new feminist politics', proceeding to observe that Diane Richardson 'similarly locates postfeminism as "feminism without the politics"' (Gwynne, 2013, p. 4). Guy Ritchie's Irene Adler constitutes a particularly clear example of this decontextualization and the way that in many twenty-first century neo-Victorian texts we apprehend the illusion of feminism without any of its import. When Adler is represented as a strong 'New Woman' there is no framing context to situate her rebelliousness as a reaction towards patriarchal strictures, she is simply independent rather than being explicitly independent of patriarchy. More troublingly, when patri-archal strictures are imposed late in the first film's narrative (with Moriarty instructing, threatening and controlling her) those positive traits evaporate: in the face of a dominant masculinity her 'strong' femininity becomes an irrelevance, confirming the notion that her strengths are independent of established hegemonic power struc-tures. Ritchie's Adler can only exhibit agency when she is allowed to, unlike Conan Doyle's Adler whose transgressive qualities are explicitly counter-hegemonic.

Notably, the treatment of Adler's character is far from unique, and perhaps the most extreme example of this tendency to valorize and then reduce progressive women concerns the character of Emily Wotton in Oliver Parker's *Dorian Gray* (2009). Significantly, here is a woman who does not appear in Oscar Wilde's source text and appears to be have been created as a means of adding a more contemporary femininity/feminism to the narrative. In Parker's adaptation, Dorian Gray lives through the final decades of the nineteenth century and into the twentieth century, growing tired of the vacuous nature of his Victorian conquests before meeting Emily. Wotton is a suffragette and possesses the same bold, wilful, independent nature as Adler. Parker often presents her seated alone or separate from the conformist crowds in order to underline her free spirit. Initially she is juxtaposed against the passive figures who have preceded her – she is invested with a bounding gait, a gleeful dynamism and an overt awareness of the potential that her 'New Womanhood' affords her. Her interest in photography underlines her status as a 'modern', superseding the classicism of the painter Basil Hallward and, more interestingly, asserting her status as bearer of the gaze, antithesis to the passive, sexualized female objects that have littered the film. However, from this point on, Wotton's narrative trajectory resembles that of Adler. As soon as she becomes romantically involved with the male protagonist her agency is utterly compromised and she is represented as both conquest and one-dimensional love interest, all strength and independence eroded.

As we have seen, in both *Sherlock Holmes* films and in *Dorian Gray* the truly problematic aspect of their gender politics only becomes visible late in the narrative arc and invariably forms part of the narrative resolution. In each of these texts the imposition of a more conservative mode of femininity occurs as part of establishing a new equilibrium, yet is almost unnoticeable as it is presented as another female identity among a plethora of identities and is situated as just another choice, with all of the concomitant agency that the word 'choice' implies. So, late in *Sherlock Holmes*, Irene Adler adopts yet another series of roles, that of damsel in distress, compliant subject and ultimately, woman in love, roles that are contextualised within the text's seeming refutation of the monolithic and the homogenous described by Genz as evidence of liberated, multi-faceted woman. The issue, however, is that the eventual assumption of these conservative, traditional roles acquires weight and force precisely because that assumption constitutes a form of conclusion late in the text, a completion of a character trajectory that takes woman from and through liberatory roles and towards a role that bears little relation to the strong, independent identities that she inhabited/played out earlier. Katie Milestone and Anneke Meyer articulate just such a scenario when, in addressing popular culture, they state that 'it appears that femininity has been diversified but that conventional notions of what it is to be feminine, helped along by postfeminism, continue powerfully to reassert themselves as the superior and appropriate type of femininity' (Milestone and Meyer, 2012, p. 213). As this idea implies, the disempowerments suffered by Adler and Emily Wotton might go unnoticed as their capitulations are rendered as a facet of diversity, and disguised by the conspicuous celebration of their strengths during the exposition and development of their characters. What becomes clear then, as these neo-Victorian works are explored in some depth, is that there is a female equivalent of the fields of masculinity argument put forward by Tony Coles in relation to masculine identities. Coles suggests that instead of there being a single hegemonic masculinity there exists a variety of dominant masculinities that men negotiate as they move between social situations (Coles, 2009). Meanwhile, in the neo-Victorian works under discussion here, there does not seem to be one dominant, hegemonic femininity and a degree of fluidity is apparent. Women are *presented* as diverse and multi-faceted, given the illusion of choice as plural identities are brought forth; however, within this plethora of femininities the one that is eventually central to narrative resolution is highly problematic. While the text points to progressive qualities, and the range of identities adopted by women seems at first glance to offer choice, possibility, freedom, independence and agency, the narrative proceeds to position this free play as, in the final analysis, 'unfulfilling' and necessarily temporary.

We might deduce then that many women in recent neo-Victorian texts enact choices that superficially signify agency and yet on closer inspection betoken a return to the strictures of traditional binaries. As such Angela McRobbie's ideas surrounding postfeminist culture are clearly borne out here. McRobbie suggests that elements of feminism have been incorporated into popular culture and emphasis frequently placed on a vocabulary of 'empowerment' 'freedom' and 'choice' (McRobbie, 2010). She asserts that these elements are then used as a substitute for feminism, offering a faux feminism rather than any real engagement with feminist politics. Key to McRobbie's argument is the idea that feminism is 'taken into account' and used as 'a signal that this is a key part of what freedom now means', with the dominant order representing itself as intrinsically progressive in its gender politics and disseminating such notions through the culture (McRobbie, 2010, p. 1). What we witness, in the many representations of twenty-first century femininities formulated within the seemingly overtly progressive female characters in these neo-Victorian fictions is just such a cultural manifestation – these women at first glance signifying the enlightened nature of the text as they embody and enact independence, agency and choice, only for that strength to be effaced. The agency these women initially assert within their respective narratives therefore might be said to constitute a form of appeasement for a supposedly enlightened mainstream audience but one that once established is almost immediately compromised and eroded through an insidious imposition of passivity, dependency and domesticity on women.

What texts such as the film adaptations of *Sherlock Holmes* and *Dorian Gray* reveal, is what Janice Doane and Devon Hodges refer to as 'the relation between the feminist project to develop an emancipatory ... rhetoric and conservative, postfeminist narratives of mass culture' (1990, p. 422). These contemporary narratives propose that emancipation has already irrefutably occurred – the early stages of the Adler and Wotton narratives clearly present this as the case – and this serves to suggest that what happens subsequently is a 'choice' made by the emancipated woman rather than a role imposed on her by a patriarchal, hegemonic status quo. The result is a conservatism legitimized by its presentation as postfeminist lifestyle choice, women using their 'empowered postfeminist position to make choices that would be regarded by many second wave feminists as problematic, located as they are in normative notions of femininity' (2006, p. 168). Here, Milestone and Meyer's words also prove pertinent: 'there is an ongoing dismantling and discrediting of feminism which offers dissenters no space for complaint' (2012, p. 212). Almost everything about these narratives cements the idea that equality has been secured, power and agency achieved; audiences are encouraged to disregard the fact that these elective 'freedoms' eventually conform to heteronormative, regressive forms of femininity and situate woman as ostensibly tamed precisely because that taming is willed by woman.

There are a range of other issues that circulate around the romantic resolutions we find in these films and that can be usefully explored through notions put forward by Rosalind Gill. Although Gill primarily discusses chick lit, due to the endemic and enduring trope of heteronormative romance within mainstream neo-Victorian fiction her ideas are apposite. Gill points out that within chick lit, the heroines 'manage to win the hero's heart in the end not because they surpass [them] in spirit or intelligence, but because they conform to traditional stereotypes of femininity' (2007, p. 237). I would suggest that the female protagonists under discussion here do both, proving themselves as just as capable as the male protagonists before their capitulation to patriarchal notions of womanhood. I would also argue that what emerges here is therefore even more disturbing than Gill suggests. The male protagonists are undoubtedly attracted to our heroines because of their non-conformative nature, but it almost seems like some form of fetishization of strength and agency that presents yet another challenge to our hero, another opportunity to prove his manhood by taming the untamable. Female independence is eroded bit by bit *until* they conform to traditional stereotypes of femininity; only then can the narrative reach resolution with a heteronormative 'happy ever after' in which, as Gill notes, the heroine actively welcomes this rescue from a life of independence and hegemonic masculinity is not only reasserted, but amplified through the unlikely nature of the conquest and the seemingly liberal nature of the man.

Tellingly, this progression through various selves and identities to reach romantic resolution is also represented as a form of personal growth, a maturation, a learning curve. The immature phase is comprised of forms of play, which are indulged in the sure and certain knowledge that the strong woman will inevitably bow under the pressures of established societal protocols and assume the heteronormative mantle. Heteronormative romance is therefore shown to be bound up with the formulation of a mature self, with the most viable gender identity being the one that fits in with the heterosexual matrix. Overall then, the power and agency that Genz accords postfeminist woman is seen by Gill as problematically conditional, with women only 'endowed with agency on condition that it is used to construct...a subject closely resembling the heterosexual male fantasy' (2007, p. 152). The fantasy is that the man of strength and the man of will can tame the untamable; if the man can dominate and subjugate his 'equal' then how strong and how manly has he proven himself to be. Furthermore, the fantasy is that the woman of strength and independence will sacrifice those freedoms for the sake of a man,offering a narrative resolution that reduces the woman's agency and choice.

By comparison, twenty-first century neo-Victorian literary texts seem to be more ideologically progressive. Certainly, recent novels such as Belinda Starling's *The Journal of Dora Damage* (2008) and John Boyne's *This House is Haunted* (2013) appear to maintain much of the pro-feminist agenda that has become synonymous with the genre through canonical twentieth century texts such as Sarah Waters's novels *Affinity, Fingersmith, Tipping the Velvet*, A. S. Byatt's *Possession*, Angela Carter's *Nights at the Circus* and Margaret Atwood's *Alias Grace*. However, I would argue that if we examine the narrative lines of these two contemporary novels in some detail we might trace a similar form of softening or dilution to that seen and described in mainstream neo-Victorian films. Indeed, though many twenty-first century neo-Victorian literary texts might construct resolutions that lack the overt entrapments, tragedies and marked shifts in character that curtail Adler and Wotton, they are not exempt from the growing sense of ideological compromise that undermines their screen counterparts.

Crucially, in the early stages of *The Journal of Dora Damage* and *This House is Haunted*, both Starling and Boyne are at pains to position compromise and conformity as social evils and to represent a woman's refusal to compromise as an admirable goal. Starling's novel uses a parable outlined in the prologue to foreground the potential dangers of such conformity:

My father used to tell me that before we are born, St Bartholomew, patron saint of bookbinders, presents our soul with a choice of two books. One is bound in the softest golden calf and majestically gold-tooled; the other is bound in plain, undyed goatskin straight from the tan-pits. Should the nascent soul choose the former, upon entering this world he will open it to find that the pages of this book are already inscribed with a story of an inescapable fate to be followed to the letter... But the pages of the latter book start off blank, and await inscription by the leading of a life of free will according to personal inspiration and divine grace. And the more one's destiny is pursued, the more brilliance the book acquires.

(Starling, 2008, p. 1)

Subsequently, Dora outlines the philosophy that she will subsequently defy. She relates one of her mother's instructions that was taught to both her and the girls in her mother's charge (noting that these dictates were never taught to the boys):

My mother advised that if one halves one's expectations, one will never be quite so disappointed. And so I learnt that a polite little girl only takes half of what she really wants, and learns to settle with that half, and so I did, especially as far as Peter and our way of life in Lambeth were concerned.

(Starling, 2008, p. 14)

Meanwhile Boyne uses the incidental figure of Miss Sharpton to similar ends, Eliza's account of this radical woman's impact upon the otherwise male Department of Entomology positioning her as a role model for our protagonist:

I rather admired Miss Sharpton and wished that I could have had the opportunity to know her better; I was aware that she had attended the Sorbonne, where she was awarded a degree, although naturally the English universities did not recognize it, and apparently her own family had cut her off on account of it. Father told me once that he had asked her whether she was looking forward to the day when she would get married and thus not have to work any more; her reply – that she would rather drink ink – had scandalized him but intrigued me.

(Boyne, 2013, p. 27)

Not only is Miss Sharpton represented as a figure of agency and uncompromising commitment in her employment, but also as a transgressive figure who pushes social boundaries in the outside world. On returning from her father's funeral, Eliza observes Miss Sharpton at the Goat and Garter public house and states:

> I had of course never entered, and was astonished to observe Miss Sharpton seated by the window, drinking a small porter and engrossed in a text book while she made notes in a jotter. Behind her I could see the expressions on the men's faces – naturally, they were appalled and assumed that she was some sort of deviant – but I suspected that their opinions would have caused her not a moment's concern. How I longed to enter that establishment and take my place beside her! Tell me, Miss Sharpton, I might have said, what shall I do with my life now?
>
> (Boyne, 2013, p. 29)

With this agenda established both novels proceed to valorize a move towards agency and both appear to inflect their Bildungsroman with the awakening of a desirable proto-feminism. So, while Starling's *The Journal of Dora Damage* may begin with a female protagonist as compromised woman, Dora is soon shown to actively resist these strictures, moving away from a number of traditional roles over the course of the narrative. She assumes the role of her husband when he becomes incapacitated by rheumatism; she must procure new clients, source materials and visit places that would not usually admit women; and she must conduct the physical labour that has hitherto been the preserve of men. Dora proves significantly more capable in these new roles than she did as a traditional domestic woman, and her newfound autonomy also leads her to new sexual knowledge and awareness of previously unexplored aspects of her character. Similarly, Boyne's Eliza Caine begins as a relatively passive figure, a dutiful daughter to a traditional father, but on his death she elects to assume a more active role as a governess at Gaudlin Hall. After leaving London she proceeds to challenge the patriarchal power structures of the Norfolk town where she is employed, questioning the dictates of its lawyers and its churchmen, defying the hysteria that has driven her predecessors from the haunted hall, growing in stature as the novel progresses.

Like Adler and Wotton, both Dora and Eliza are juxtaposed against more traditional (compromised) women and this knowledge frames the resolutions of the novels, encouraging the reader to interpret the final moments of these texts as victories for progressive femininity.

Dora is set against a cast of women including Mrs Eeles, the perpetual Victorian mourner dressed in black, Lady Sylvia Knightley, an upper class abolitionist who is nevertheless entirely out of touch with the realities of the day, and Agatha Marrow, embodiment of traditional matriarchy. Amidst these women Dora's progressive credentials and her ability to assume a range of diverse roles appear more marked and admirable. Meanwhile, as a heroic, indomitable and resilient governess confronting dark, supernatural forces that have destroyed the six women that have preceded her in her position, Eliza's survival must surely be read as an endorsement of the strong, independent, outspoken new femininity she has acquired as the narrative has progressed. However, the problematic aspects of both *Dora Damage* and *This House is Haunted* lie in the nature of these resolutions or the terms of their victories. So, while Starling links Dora's newfound agency (as she acts to save the business and the family home) to liberation and personal growth it is important to note that in actively staving off threat she is first and foremost protecting her daughter Lucinda: Dora's progressive energies are blended with maternal instinct and her heterogeneity can be viewed as a temporary state designed to facilitate domestic and familial stability. A mess of contradictions emerges, with Dora frequently finding herself caught between conflicting traditional femininities. When she is not being a 'good wife' she is still being a 'good mother', the irony being that Dora's move away from the archetypes of angel of the hearth and passive domestic woman are nevertheless contextualized by her adherence to another trope of traditional femininity, every subversive act constituting an equal and opposite form of conformity to the doxa. Notably, this same tension between progressive attitudes and compromise is seen in the awakening of Dora's desire through the pornography that she later destroys: she awakens sexually through the pornographic material she binds, and through her encounters with the new masculinity of Din, but then denies herself the active sexual liberation that Lady Sybil allows herself, electing instead to pursue maternal love and female companionship. Similarly, despite her physical bravery, daring and fortitude Eliza requires the spirit of her deceased father to intercede and save her in *This House is Haunted*'s denouement and furthermore, her victory will be rewarded by a return to traditional feminine pleasures as she effectively becomes a mother to the orphaned Eustace.

What we see in Dora and Eliza is an endorsement of a relatable form of modern femininity, and unlike the films addressed earlier, a strength that is sustained in resolutions that reward the female protagonist's influence, capability and stoicism. Nevertheless, despite the fact that these novels provide more palatable resolutions and avoid the heterosexual romance that diminishes Adler and Wotton they still fall short of the uncompromising radicalism they initially vaunt in Starling's prologue and through Boyne's Miss Sharpton, as their protagonists move towards relative normalcy. The issue is not that we fail to see exceptional women in these texts, on the contrary, these women are present and celebrated. The problem is a reversal of the narrative trajectory seen in twentieth-century examples of the genre. In canonical neo-Victorian works there is a move from normalcy to exception, a move which is subverted in the decisions Dora and Eliza ultimately make as they choose normalcy as their reward. Otherness as starting point lacks the radical power of otherness as sign of maturation. Consequently, when read against or in relation to their Victorian hypotexts, fictions such as *Dora Damage* and *This House is Haunted* bear the hallmarks of the truly progressive text (revelling as they do in exceptional female figures) but read against twentieth century neo-Victorian antecedents they are still marked by the feeling that the gender politics proclaimed in their expositional phases have been diluted, as exception is represented as a developmental stage in the path to a homogenous, monolithic and markedly more conventional identity.

What *Sherlock Holmes, Dorian Gray, The Journal of Dora Damage, This House is Haunted* and many other twenty-first century neo-Victorian works reveal is that the very interplay between traditionalism and radicalism that has so often facilitated the representation of progressive gender politics as laudable and necessary might also serve markedly more regressive ends. We should begin to confront the idea that texts that continue to produce images of female empowerment and appear to form part of an ongoing, progressive process, in fact frequently disavow that process and, more troublingly, efface the sense of it being necessary. The irony of the twenty-first century texts addressed here is that they stage a narrative journey from exception (defined by markers of empowerment and independence) to normalcy (defined by behaviours in keeping with traditional models of ideal femininity), yet disguise that transition in the trappings of a genre so often valorized for precisely the opposite narrative trajectory, masking lapses into hegemonic conformity behind a masquerade of postfeminist play.

Seen in this light the nature of the genre's use of the Victorian milieu becomes highly problematic. While this milieu can constitute the backdrop against which women like Irene Adler and Emily Wotton initially stand out in admirably sharp relief, it can, conversely, operate as marker of those women's unsustainable difference from the status quo; it can thus serve to justify any conservative step back towards the centre ground of a traditional gender identity as fitting and understandable. In other words, the Victorian milieu in these contemporary fictions can present the regressive choices these women ultimately make as an inevitable return, with the past figured in these fictions acting as a context in which the progressive energies of women such as Adler and Wotton are positioned as different, other, exceptional, briefly out of step and therefore prone to what the texts suggest is an entirely natural suspension.

Clearly these ideas are relevant to our present and Milestone and Meyer have asserted that we frequently witness in postfeminist returns to traditional modes and values 'a return to earlier ways of thinking about femininity ... Women are given more options of identity, but at the same time the conventional feminine identity is often framed as the most valid, appropriate and good one' (2012, p. 93). Recent neo-Victorian works offer just such an illusory diversity followed by (to varying degrees and in varying forms) the re-imposition of a doxological Victorian femininity. This retrograde step not only reveals the disturbing propensity of our contemporary culture to gravitate towards a regressive gender politics, but also the ability of the Victorian milieu to camouflage and validate that return beneath a crinoline verisimilitude and the recapitulation of the ideologically 'authentic' traditional gender politics enshrined in Barthes's doxological Victorian. Tellingly, Imelda Whelehan has stated that 'the use of retro imagery and nostalgia is a key device in the construction of the new sexism', proceeding to note that 'referencing a previous era, embracing its iconography, becomes an important way of suggesting that sexism is safely sealed in the past, while constructing scenarios that would draw condemnation if they were regarded as contemporary' (2004). Whelehan believes that evoking nostalgia often forestalls criticism and I would argue that these concerns are borne out in neo-Victorian texts that might lack overt back-lash, contain narrative acts and images that celebrate the strengths of New Women and yet disguise conservatism and legitimize hege-mony through the tropes of the past they conjure. These are fictions that further forestall criticism as they superficially appear beyond reproach, their problems are more difficult to discern, a fact exac-erbated by the feeling that many of the troubling aspects of their gender politics involve dilution rather than explicit effacement. Indeed, many of the issues raised by recent neo-Victorian fictions are epitomised by the suggestion made by Dora Damage's mother: '[W]hatever it is that you desire, halve it.' Her reductive decision to favour pragmatism over idealism finds its correlative in the mod-ificationof a revisionist genre while the consequences of this shift can be seen in the curtailment of those progressive femininities that fleetingly seemed to have it all.

Note

1. Simon Joyce (2007) *The Victorians in the Rearview Mirror*. Ohio: Ohio University Press, p. 6.

   Barthes notes the perpetuation of a commonsensical 'doxa' of public opinion regarding the Victorians. Barthes has stated that the 'basic shape of the doxalogical Victorian' remains a structuring ever-present within our culture.

Primary texts

Boyne, John (2013) *This House is Haunted*. London: Doubleday.
Conan Doyle, Arthur (2012) *The Five Orange Pips and Other Cases*. London: Penguin.
Dorian Gray. Directed by Oliver Parker (2009) Momentum Pictures.
Sherlock Holmes. Directed by Guy Ritchie (2009) Warner Bros Pictures.
Sherlock Holmes: A Game of Shadows. Directed by Guy Ritchie (2011). Warner Bros. Pictures.
Starling, Belinda (2008) *The Journal of Dora Damage*. London: Bloomsbury Publishing.

Bibliography

Coles, Tony (2009) 'Negotiating the field of masculinity: The production and reproduction of multiple dominant masculinities', *Men and Masculinities*, 12(1), October 2009, pp. 30–44.

Doane, Janice and Devon Hodges (1990) 'Undoing feminism: From the preoedipal to postfeminism in Anne Rice's vampire chronicles', *American Literary History*, 2(3), p. 422.

Genz, Stephanie (2010) 'Singled out: Postfeminism's "New Woman" and the dilemma of having it all', *The Journal of Popular Culture*, 43(1), 2010, pp. 97–119.

Gill, Rosalind (2006) 'Postfeminist media culture: Elements of a sensibility', *European Journal of Cultural Studies*, 10(2), pp. 14–166.

Gill, Rosalind (2007) *Gender and the Media*. Cambridge: Polity Press.

Gwynne, Joel (2013) *Postfeminism and Contemporary Hollywood Cinema*. Basingstoke: Palgrave Macmillan.

Joyce, Simon (2007) *The Victorians in the Rearview Mirror*. Ohio: Ohio University Press.

King, Jeanette (2005) *The Victorian Woman Question in Contemporary Feminist Fiction*. Basingstoke: Palgrave Macmillan.

McRobbie, Angela (2010) *The Aftermath of Feminism: Gender, Culture and Social Change*. London: Sage Publications.

Milestone, Katie and Anneke Meyer (2012) *Gender and Popular Culture*. Cambridge: Polity Press.

Whelehan, Imelda (2004) *Having It All (Again?)*, Available online at: www.docin.com/p-99447553.html

Index

Note: The locators followed by the letter 'n' refer notes.

CPSIA information can be obtained
at www.ICGtesting.com
Printed in the USA
LVOW13*2346020417
529377LV00015B/283/P